Contents

Dedication

To our children Fenix and Salome for giving us the opportunity to be parents and guiding us on this path of change to have a positive influence on their lives and formation.

To God because he is our greatness and thanks to him we have been able to complete this process by giving us intelligence, wisdom and patience.

Walter Murillo
Yeimy Serrato

Atenti, a pedagogical tool to improve the attentional process

Management of ADHD, an integral vision in the classroom

ScienciaScripts

Cover image: www.ingimage.com

This book is a translation from the original published under ISBN 978-3-659-06162-2.

Publisher:
Sciencia Scripts
is a trademark of
Dodo Books Indian Ocean Ltd. and OmniScriptum S.R.L publishing group

120 High Road, East Finchley, London, N2 9ED, United Kingdom
Str. Armeneasca 28/1, office 1, Chisinau MD-2012, Republic of Moldova, Europe

ISBN: 978-620-6-85366-4

Acknowledgements

To our children, forgers of unique experiences and main protagonists of the book.

To our parents who have forged resilient human beings and in one way or another contributed to the development of the academic process.

Summary

Attention deficit is growing more and more in educational contexts, due to the lack of medical detection and early approach to disorders such as ADHD (Attention Deficit Hyperactivity Disorder), this disorder without proper attention can generate severe sequelae in adolescence and adulthood in different contexts of life, Due to this, the attentional pedagogical strategy ATENTI is created, which links some contents supported by a virtual learning environment that favours the attentional processes of children at early ages within the educational context.

In the research the relevance and validation of the strategy is verified from two perspectives, the first begins with a pedagogical level through the validation of the contents of two experts related to educational psycho-iography and subsequently, a technological validation of functionality and relevance through two experts in virtual education and digital content, to subsequently involve a population of cycle 1 of an IED of Bogota and evaluate the impact of the strategy in the attentional aspect.

The present research is based on a qualitative method with an exploratory scope that validates the strategy with a thorough scientific argumentation of the contents articulated with the interface of the virtual learning environment and the field process with the children.

Key words:

Attention, Neuroplasticity, ADHD, Play, Physical Activity, cognitive processes.

4

1 Problem Statement

Attention Deficit Hyperactivity Disorder (ADHD) is considered a popular disorder in children, however, its diagnosis in Latin America is still linked to medical evaluations, which prevents more cases from being detected in contexts such as the classrooms of district schools, where a large percentage of parents do not have the facilities to have a thorough medical follow-up in which they can define criteria for thinking that the child has ADHD (Salamanca L, 2014). (ADHD is defined as a disorder measured by scales, however the primary focus is on the attentional processes of the children with a more precise approach in the school environment, since 70% of those established as inattentive present learning deficits while the remaining 30% have behavioural problems (Rodrigue/. E. N., 2006), hence the importance of establishing intervention schemes for the approach in the school environment at an early age, which would benefit their academic relationship with their biological development through an optimal process.

In the classroom, the development of children with the syndrome can affect their social and academic life, as they develop activities and behaviours that, as mentioned by (Mena B, 2006), affect the free development of the pedagogical processes and other spaces where the children develop, therefore the importance of establishing an extra help in the learning and motor process is evident.

In the local context, education has a defined structure and very specific parameters in terms of what is to be obtained pedagogically from the children, as a scope of the educational process in early childhood, for this reason the proposals that underlie the conventional process, forge a fundamental path in support of the cognitive development of the child in the attentional aspect, carrying out the appropriate follow-up and approach in articulation with traditional education.

The individualisation of learning in the curricular structure for students with inclusion monitoring established by the Ministry of National Education is not framed within the pedagogical support documents (curricular guidelines, basic learning rights, among other national guidelines), This does not facilitate some cognitive processes of children in early childhood, and further strengthens the need to support pedagogical strategies that favour interdisciplinary processes where the family context and the school are articulated, focusing on them as safe and trusting environments for children.

Within the framework of the institutional educational project of each school, the approach to the population with special needs should be clearly defined within the reasonable adjustments, flexible curriculum and PIAR mentioned in Decree 1421 of 2017, which impact in a certain way on the micro-curricular by having to adapt strategies and learning times, on the meso-curricular by adapting the scope of academic objectives within the pedagogical space and on the macro-curricular by establishing general actions for the attention of the inclusion population, facing a general change and adaptation within the institutional academic processes, thinking about equity, permanence and accessibility, as well as the support of alternative strategies as a support to their cognitive development, all of the above taking into account that the population, especially in early childhood, is totally heterogeneous, both in processes and in cognitive development and as an entity in formation should be a recurrent premise of updating in the administrative and pedagogical processes of each institution.

In South America, the increase in the prevalence of Attention Deficit Hyperactivity Disorder (ADHD) is well above average, and Colombia specifically has the highest prevalence rate in the world (Llanos, Garcia, Gonzalez, & Puentes, 2019). Puentes, 2019) and this, without counting that the means and methods of detection are still precarious and the contexts do not contribute to detect it in time, this due to the economic difficulties and pedagogy in the characteristics of the disorder, this is supported by a study conducted by the University of Rosario in the year 2014, where it is evident that more than half of the cases studied present one of the two conditions, that is, they have attentional difficulties or hyperactivity, concluding the importance of detecting it at an early age in order to make the appropriate medical and pedagogical approaches to improve their condition in the futureLaisuue (2014) taken from (Eltiempo, 2014); which sets alarm bells ringing in educational entities, and as a consequence, the pedagogical processes that should be carried out with this type of population, favouring their processes and conditions in other contexts.

Since 2008, the importance of an early approach to the disorder and its efficacy in treatment has been emphasised, otherwise the consequences in adolescence and adulthood can be considerable, leading to behaviour and difficulties in specific contexts.

In the educational context of the official schools, in a subjective way, the important attentional difficulties that the children have in the first stages of education can be evidenced, together with the lack of structure in processes or strategies of individualised intervention to the characteristics of each case, intervention must be structured as it is a disorder that affects the complex neuropsychological development, which varies according to each child, and also alters important developmental processes to perform activities in a "normal" environment (Quintanar, Gomez, Solovieva, & Bonilla, 2011). Bonilla, 2011)

"The functional weakness of some brain sectors has a systemic effect on the child's activity and, in general, on the development of all spheres of the child's psychic, cognitive, affective, emotional, motivational and personality life" (Quintanar, Gomez, Solovieva, & Bonilla, 2011). The quality of life that should be evidenced in adulthood, frames the development from the first years of life, understanding as such, the importance that determines the early and precise approach of each case detected with attention deficit or hyperactivity disorder, and also, the support of attentional strategies, as a determining factor in the processes of cognitive development and neuroplasticity, which contribute in the pedagogical structures with activities focused on strengthening the different types of attention and the contexts to use them.

Once the social problem to be addressed and the need for a safe, reliable strategy that is articulated with the academic environment, but above all inclusive and easily accessible to all types of population, supporting the psychosocial conditions, the specificity of the research proposal arises, The specific nature of the research proposal, an attentional pedagogical strategy mediated by technology as a plus of activation in the cognitive processes of the participating children, favouring the contexts in which they interact, understanding the need to carry out a sustainable proposal that essentially favours human development in all aspects of the children of early childhood in the schools of the district; Given the above, the question arises, £ What is the impact of a technological tool in the attentional process derived from a pedagogical strategy?

Objectives

General objective

To evaluate a technological tool as a pedagogical strategy to improve the attentional process in children.

Specific objectives

• To identify characteristics of ADHD that may affect educational performance in the attentional aspect by means of reliable studies and appropriate literature.

• To design a technological tool that allows the students of cycle 1 of the IED Bravo Paez to improve the attentional processes.

• To evaluate the changes presented in the attentional process of the students of cycle 1 of the IED Bravo Paez in order to identify the impact of the tool.

Justification

In the immediate clinical context, the criteria for measuring the cognitive actions of children with the disorder in their attentional, hyperactivity or combined difficulties are not well defined, due to the fact that the behaviours and symptoms are variable according to each case and are accentuated or triggered depending on the context that surrounds them or where they link their cognitive and social development; firstly, the concepts of hyperactivity mentioned by (Vaquerizo, 2005), which establishes a behavioural disorder that makes it difficult to carry out normal socialisation actions with many interruptions in the communicative processes affecting other scenarios of development, therefore their cognitive and personal maturity is affected in the essential stages of human development, are clarified; secondly, the importance of the attentional processes in learning, socialisation, understanding of the context where it develops and the appropriation of new forms of the world is taken into account, adding to the attentional processes together with perception and memory, fundamental aspects for mediations in the cognitive development of the child (Ocampo, 2011).Therefore, and understanding that the first educational stages where the processes of readiness, gross motor skills, fine motor skills and the acquisition of discipline, among other processes, are developed, are essential to strengthen neural networks correctly stimulated through play and playfulness, methods conducive to establish assertive relationships with children. It mentions (Fundacioncadah.org, 2012) the benefits and stimuli that are developed in each brain area, 1. in the Sensory Area: senses and perception; Motor Area: fine motor skills, gross motor skills and proprioception; 2. Cognitive Area: memory, attention, cognition, logical processing;3. Communicative area: language, expression, interaction, dialogues, rituals; 4. Affective area: overcoming fears, anxieties, phobias; Social area: roles, competence, conflict resolution.

In this way, the importance and convenience of the ATENTI pedagogical strategy is detailed, using play and playfulness as a bridge to strengthen the attentional processes of the areas of work previously mentioned, supporting cognitive development and neuroplasticity from a pleasant and safe environment for children and tutors.

The family context and school dynamics are the most affected within a more structured process in the treatment of Attention Deficit Hyperactivity Disorder (ADHD) or simply in the failure to detect it in time, which in the long term generates greater difficulties in family dynamics and educational contexts, This, without referring to other social dynamics in which he/she will be involved as an adolescent or adult, affecting the possibilities, by having to allocate more money in a successful approach to the disorder when the child or adolescent is older (Pinto, Melia, & Miranda, 2009), another important argument in this regard is the fact that the child or adolescent is not able to meet the academic objectives and learning processes in a normal way, without referring to other social dynamics in which he/she will be involved when he/she is an adolescent or adult. Miranda, 2009), another important argument to affirm the fundamental role that the strategy plays in the educational and family context, as well as being inclusive, by making it possible for any type of population to have access to the contents regardless of their economic or social position, thus consolidating itself as a proposal with a social impact.

The success of the process depends firstly on the articulation of the actors involved in the process, children, tutors, teachers, creators of the strategy and other participants, and secondly on the support that can be given by the medical concepts about the real conditions of the child, in terms of diagnosis, precise approaches and special needs of each case, in this respect the family plays the primary role in the first stage which is the early detection of the disorder. In the practical action, playful activities and interactive games will be articulated from the perspective of gamification (educational context), all this mediated by a virtual learning environment, which meets all the necessary parameters of linkage to a conventional curriculum under any pedagogical model, i.e., the strategy is reliable and articulating conventional education in the initial cycles of any school,

By resorting to the literature for the review of the relevance of the pedagogical strategy, the importance of play and playfulness in the cognitive development and motor processes of children is reinforced, an importance that is contributed from any context where it interacts; On the other hand, it is indisputable to frame the precipitous increase of the cases of diagnosed children, without counting those who do not have access to an adequate health system, which makes it difficult to have accurate figures and an adequate early treatment, making it difficult for school and low socio-economic contexts to have access to strategies of prevention and action of attentional contents.

The research proposal structures a process designed with activities focused on the different types of attention, moments designed to favour cognitive and motor development, always bearing in mind the need to articulate the strategy in an educational context, where tools and actors are provided to favour each moment and each context in which the children interact, understanding that the adequate and early approach will guarantee a considerable improvement according to the conditions of the attentional deficit of each case. In this sense, what is achieved in the first stages of human development will have an impact on the family, social and educational contexts as the child grows older and his or her cognitive processes require more stimuli to achieve an adequate social and personal adaptation to each need.

2 Theoretical and referential framework

Background

Spain is one of the countries in the world with the greatest approach and studies in relation to the diagnosis and treatment of Attention Deficit Hyperactivity Disorder (ADHD), in terms of history, the first who spoke of something similar, was Dr. Alexander Crichton in 1798, describing symptoms similar to those known today, in relation in 1845 the psychiatrist Heinrich Hoffmanna contributes greatly to the process, when in one of his publications he announces symptoms defined as hyperactive, impulsive and scattered, concepts that for the time generated quite a lot of eloquence with descriptions of the disorder, impulsive and dispersed, concepts that for that time generated a lot of eloquence with the descriptions of the disorder, but it is not until 1902 when the doctor George Frederic Stillpadre of paediatrics makes a very accurate scientific description of the symptoms and conditions of the children that for that time were denominated defect of moral control, and seen as a behavioural alteration in boys and girls, one of them identified as punctual alterations of attention and hyperactivity. The diagnostic conditions of ADHD have been studied for decades, defined before the emergence of contemporary psychiatry and using almost the same tools for symptom detection (Quintero & Castano, 2014).

Continuing in the international context with scientific advances and understanding that ADHD is a neurodevelopmental disorder and can affect the contexts in which children develop, in 2014 it became scientifically evident that this disorder should be addressed in early stages and that boys have higher statistics than girls, affecting cognitive, academic, social and family functioning, The statistics (Table 1) show that since 2001, efforts have been made in these countries to detect the disorder (Hidalgo & Sanchez, 2014), and that the most industrialised countries have implemented clinical practices that support the work of diagnosis, evidencing the exponential growth of the disorder and its poor treatment approach. Sanchez, 2014)

Table 1 *Attention Deficit Hyperactivity Disorder Clinical Practice Guidelines*

Tabla I. Guías de práctica clínica del trastorno por déficit de atención e hiperactividad		
Organismo	**País**	**Fecha publicación**
American Academy of Pediatrics (AAP)	EE.UU.	2001, 2005, 2011
Cincinnati Children's Hospital Medical Center	EE.UU	2004
European Society for Child and Adolescent Psychiatry (ESCAP)	Unión Europea	2004
European Child & Adolescent Psychiatry	Unión Europea	2006
The Texas Children's Medication Algorithm (Texas)	EE.UU.	2006
American Academy of Child and Adolescent Psychiatry (AACAP)	EE.UU.	2007
Institute for clinical Systems Improvement (ICSI)	EE.UU.	2007
National Institute for Health and Clinical Excellence (NICE)	Reino Unido	2009, 2013
Canadian ADHD Practice Guidelines (CADDRA)	Canadá	2008, 2011
Scottish Intercollegiate Guidelines Network (SIGN)	Reino Unido	2005, 2009
Royal Australasian College of Physicians (RACP)	Australia	2009
Guía de Práctica Clínica del Sistema Nacional de Salud	España	2010

In the last 20 years in the United States the diagnosis of ADHD has multiplied by 6, and these alarming figures have turned the childhood disorder into the main method of consultation of children, depending on the context and the environment, the figures have increased due to the studies and specific tests that have been implemented in the American community, As mentioned by (Hergueras, 2016) the use of specific criteria increase the reliability and recurrence of positive tests for the disorder, so it is vital to be able to make an immediate approach and in the first years of schooling, this in order to establish the mechanisms of action and control to promote their social and academic development.

At the local level, Latin American meetings have been taking place, which have framed the importance of establishing adequate care programmes for children with disabilities.

ADHD, since, as mentioned in the Cartagena declaration for ADHD, it is on the list of mental health problems due to the social and school repercussions they present, and also shows that at least thirty-six million people in Latin America have the disorder and of these only 23% have adequate treatment support, which sets alarm bells ringing in terms of the projects that must be advanced to ensure the minimum intervention to recover their health and well-being in the process of evolution of their lives (De la Pena, Palacio, & Barragan, 2010). Barragan, 2010).

One of the most specific studies was carried out in Bogota, especially in public and public schools where 1100 boys and girls between the ages of 4 and 14 years were tested, resulting in a prevalence of 57% positive of the total number of children who participated, hyperactivity is the least predominant during the study, while of the total percentage, inattention leads the results according to the scales of the disorder in children and 5 year olds, with the male gender predominating over the female (Velez, Talero, Gonzalez, & Ibanez, 2008), which frames the importance of the development of the present work and its investigation of how to improve the attentional processes in children of cycle 1 through activities related to physical education. Ibanez, 2008), which frames the importance of the development of the present work and its investigation of how to improve the attentional processes in children of cycle 1 by means of activities related to physical education.

For 2016, some considerations on the aetiopathogenesis and treatment of Attention Deficit Hyperactivity Disorder (ADHD) are shown, which favour daily activities and actions in each context of life, with the fundamental objective of measurements to alleviate the disorder and the information associated with the morbidities and conceptual approaches with the effect on other systems. In the approach to detect the conditions of each individual, some essential parameters are established for their detection, these parameters relating hereditary, acquired biological, neorophysiological, genetic, psychosocial and environmental, neurochemical and neuroanatomical factors, which further frames the spectrum within the detection of cases in early childhood with positive influences on their diagnosis and early approach, however although there are many more topics to address within their detection, the treatment continues to comply with the schemes established since the beginning of the twentieth century, a multidisciplinary approach is the most appropriate with or without medication and its main idea is to impact on cognitive, behavioural and social functions, among other measures it is important to continue with treatment in all aspects of life without neglecting sport, nutrition, planned routines etc., This is due to the fact that without a previous and adequate approach during the early stages of the child's development, adaptive problems of drug use, sexual risk behaviours and dissocial behaviours will occur during adolescence, which will have a negative impact on their family, educational and personal context (Portela, Carbonell, Hechavarria, & Jacas, 2016). Jacas, 2016).

The educational context, focusing on attentional and hyperactivity processes in academic actions (Mena, 2017) exposes the difficulties presented by teachers when planning and executing classes with the population detected with the disorder, and proposes actions and strategies to address these processes in an effective way to move from a "concern" to an "occupation" as stated in his article; to reach the solution or management, we must first refer to how the academic processes are impacted by the symptoms of the disorder according to the cases in which they affect attentional processes, hyperactivity or combined, in other words, the approaches are divided according to the behaviours presented, for attentional processes due to lack of apprehension of knowledge, it is recommended to develop a programme accompanied by constant tutoring, In the case of hyperactivity, the same behaviours are managed by adding a control in the rules and habits, all of this focused on the academic processes in the classroom and outside of it, in addition to the teachers playing a fundamental role in the process, it is important to emphasise their importance by understanding their needs and looking for teaching alternatives to get the best potential out of the children.

Through a literature review conducted in 2018, the main elements of the diagnosis and treatment since

1999 were highlighted, this review was conducted in repositories of regional journals and internet articles, which aims to collect over the years the main topics in common with respect to the characteristics of diagnosis and treatment; It is agreed that the diagnosis is clinical and its early detection is essential to take the necessary actions to reduce the symptoms and their social impact. In order to obtain greater reliability in the diagnosis, a process of interviews supported by instruments is required. The clinical interview should be the first to give its opinion of the case, then there will be direct contact with the parents and the child, followed by the most suitable evaluation scales determined by the professional in charge of the process, At the same time and parallel to the interviews, neurological studies are carried out to show the common alterations among the population with ADHD. Once all the processes have been carried out and a more precise detection has been made, the most appropriate treatment for each case is given, which must be individual and then introduced in its social component. Within the approach, an intervention of specialists such as psychologists, psychopedagogues, neurologists, psychiatrists, defectologists, occupational therapists, speech therapists and, in short, any professional who favours their development (Francia, Migues, & Penalver, 2018) is conceived. The most favourable context and where treatment can be better measured is the academic context, due to the activities that are developed there and the contextual processes that connect the child with psychomotor development.

In 2019 at the paediatric update congress, some studies were shared with the most recent updates on the management of ADHD, affirming the alteration that is caused in the child in some brain regions mainly originated by genetic components that alter their neurodevelopment presenting the symptoms of the disorder, in addition between 6 and 7 years is the ideal age for detection as they begin to mature the structures that regulate attention and it is essential to address it from an early age to avoid reaching adolescence without adequate and controlled treatment. They also coincide with a long-term multimodal treatment consisting of 1. pharmacology, 2. intensive behavioural treatment, 3. combined treatment between 1 and 2, 4. treatment as usual in the community which acts as a control group. After the detection and the assignment of the appropriate multimodal treatment, they carried out a follow-up of 14 months, then 2 to 3 years, 6 to 8 years, 10 to 14 years after the start of the study respectively, which concludes with a rate of asymptomatic control ADHD with respect to those who never had a treatment or early detection, in short, the gold standard is the multimodal treatment that has presented strong results over the years mitigating the impact of the context where it interacts (Quintero F., 2019). With regard to the control of interference in 2019 a literature review was conducted on the performance in the tasks that evaluate the control of interference in children with ADHD, the method used was a descriptive analysis of 33 articles and 520 identified, after performing the analysis of the literature it is deduced that children with ADHD have the control of interference alteado with a tendency to present lower successes, On the other hand, the review pointed out an alteration in the patterns of neuronal activation and inhibitory controls and relation in the processing of stimuli, which supports the reliability of an alteration in the control of interference, which finally impacts on school processes due to their alterations in the following of rules and control of emotions in every aspect of school. These processes when detected can be addressed by means of the treatment indicated in each case after detection, in summary, interference controls is a process that is evaluated by means of specific tests that show the areas where the brain alters the processes of "normal" development of the child (Jimenez, Jose, & Restrepo, 2019).Within the detection processes, it is evident that the strength of the processes linked to images or neurological studies is evident, as these give a little more precision about the deficiencies in brain functions that will be provided as a determinant in their treatment, This is due to the complexity and concern of parents about the medication for its long-term side effects, hence all the new studies contribute to a more precise detection and approach to the disorder with the sole purpose of providing the best possibilities and quality of life in all contexts to children who are diagnosed with ADHD.

Conceptual Framework

In the following, the main concepts taken into account for the specific approach of the research proposal will be mentioned, carrying out a specific revision, triangulating the concepts according to their importance.

ADHD

Attention deficit hyperactivity disorder is defined as a "neurodevelopmental disorder characterised by a pattern of behaviour and cognitive functioning, which can evolve over time and is likely to cause difficulties in cognitive, educational and/or occupational functioning" (Quintero & Castano, 2014). Castano, 2014), defined within three scales or patterns of recognition that frame the prevalence according to the case and its possible approach, the first is the inattentive child which generates educational and social processes that are difficult to empathise with, in addition to being a passive child with little interest in the tasks assigned to him, distracted and not very careful with his things, he is usually forgetful and does not seem to listen when they are talking to him, he is easily distracted and does not manage to have a sustained mental effort in school activities, The second is the child with hyperactivity who does not manage to generate an adequate space to be quiet, is inappropriate for games, often gets up from his chair, interrupts conversations, finds it difficult to sit down to perform certain tasks and the most serious is when he presents aggressive manifestations within his contexts, and finally there is the convergence of the two stages which generate more specific clinical intervention topics due to the particularity of each case (Mena, Nicolau, Salat, Tort, & Romero, 2006). Romero, 2006).

Within the epidemiology of ADHD there is a prevalence of close to 10% in the total preschool population, with a predominant incidence in children, and although its validity is still being questioned due to the lack of precise analytical or imaging tests, it continues to be a purely clinical diagnosis, studies since the beginning of the 19th century show the high prevalence in diagnoses worldwide, and seen from various perspectives that combine in arguments to define it as a disorder that markedly affects children, affecting their educational, family and social development. Seen from the etiopathogenesis and entering into specificity, the disorder does not have a single cause, but different factors emerge that affect according to each situation, there are neurochemical factors with alterations in neurotransmitters such as dopamine and noradrenaline, which have a direct incidence within the attentional processes and hyperactivity, This according to each function, that is to say that linked to the attentional processes is noradrenaline and to hyperactivity is adrenaline and from them an alteration of regulatory pathways according to each case, in addition, another factor that has been studied to detect precisely the disorder is the neuroanatomical one, in which there is a significantly lower activity of the volume of the dorsolateral prefrontal cortex and regions connected to it, as a result of a subsequent neuroimaging and which as a conclusion shows the differences in brain activities of children with ADHD, Another factor that contains an approximate incidence of 75% in detected cases is the genetic and neurobiological with which the prevalence can vary according to environmental and psychosocial factors that can modulate their characteristics according to the impact on developmental processes and other processes that to date identify each test (Quintero & Castano, 2014). Castano, 2014).

For the detection of ADHD, it starts with a series of tests that are established in a clinical manner, according to the prevalence of symptoms in each context and with specific actions, and also measured by different criteria such as age, symptomatogenesis, pervasiveness and diffusion, in order to specify a clinical picture and give a specific evaluation as the only reliable way to approve a diagnosis with differential prevalence; the support and information collected from parents and teachers is fundamental to determine the strengths and weaknesses in each individual and thus be able to analyse the most suitable approach for each case, (Rohde, Buitelaar, Gerlach, & Faraone, 2019), an approach that must be provided under the guidance of an interdisciplinary team that favours the disadvantages presented in the diagnosis and on the contrary strengthens the psychosocial perspectives that determine a future and a development according to the needs of the context.

One of the fundamental points in the intervention and approach to ADHD is the socialisation of the family, teachers and patients about the disorder, in order to strengthen social ties and avoid prejudices in the treatment of this complex disorder. This education goes hand in hand with clinical and psychosocial intervention, interventions that, if necessary, articulate medication and other processes that improve executive functions, behavioural and cognitive management appropriate to each case. As the disorder is complex, in the approach to ADHD the actions are aimed at the management of the symptoms, and for this, it is essential to take into account what type of interventions and what focuses will be the most appropriate, and this varies according to each case. The work must be continuous, without failing to perceive the determinant actions of human development, that is to say, that during childhood the correct approach is fundamental to avoid greater complications in the symptoms in adolescence or adulthood (Rohde, Buitelaar, Gerlach, & Faraone, 2019).

Another established source in the detection of the disorder is neuropsychology which, as the science in charge of brain-behaviour articulation, has contributed the most important processes within the detection of ADHD, and is also the science that explores more precisely the profile and situation of each detected case. Therefore, it is essential to address issues related to the attentional processes in children with signs of ADHD, in order to establish the technical improvements that can be found within the cognitive process of children in activities that can focus their attentional processes in the classroom.

The causes of the origin of ADHD converge in a biological vulnerability that interacts with other aspects to develop its determined prevalence, among these vulnerabilities we find neurochemical and neuroanatomical factors that do not allow adequate brain regulation and activation in some cognitive processes, on the other hand, the genetic factor frames a 75% of heritability which can be modulated by environmental and social influences in the cases detected, this articulating the aspects of the origin and resulting in an effective diagnosis (Quintero & Castano, 2014).

For children with ADHD, the methodological approach must be adapted to the environments in the primary approach process, environments such as the home and school are considered to be primordial and should be given special consideration in order to contribute to the development processes from all areas, and as such, from the psychosocial contribution, the results will be more important (Mena, Nicolau, Salat, Tort, & Romero, 2006).

Attentional Processes

"Attention is the process of orienting the mind to an exclusive object. Attention is a focus of observation that is somehow given to us. While we are awake, we are attentive to whatever it [whatever it is] is, even if it [whatever it is] changes every six seconds. In a manner of speaking, attention is the only representative that consciousness has" (Lopez L. , 2018), hence the importance that attention imposes on the defining mental processes, such as concentration and consciousness, for this reason the impulses and processes that are determined by means of good attention emphasise the importance of the object of study of this project.

There is an important variability in response times measured with functional magnetic resonance imaging that determines a relatively low spontaneous frequency in the functioning of the brain in everyday activities that lead us to think about the behavioural changes of children with ADHD measuring attentional processes and hyper;icdvid;id(G;ircf;i & De la torre, 2013), these behavioural changes are those that determine the field of action in the school processes of boys and girls, which focus efforts on being able to intervene in a precise and effective way the attentional processes with the link that can be generated in all the contexts where the child develops, as a complement, the relationship between the academic processes in children of cycle 1 with their cognitive development is established, since if it is not possible to focus these attentional processes at an appropriate age they could generate an increase in the conditions of the disorder.

In order to allow a more precise approach, it is essential to know the types of attention that are expressed in an individual during the development of different activities (see Table 2),

Table 2 Types *of care according to internal and external modules*

Criteria	Types of care	Description	Example
Origin and nature of the spherules	Internal	Refers to the individual's ability to attend to his or her own mental processes o any interoceptive stimulation.	physical sensations that take place in a state of relaxation

13

			The sounds of vehicular traffic, when the individual is driving.
	External	Refers to that which is picked up by any external stimulus	
Subject's attitude	Volunteer	It depends on the individual's decision to focus on a specific activity.	Pay attention when someone is teaching us how to do something.
	Involuntary	Depends on the force with which the stimulus reaches the subject	Turn towards the place where a loud sound is generated.
Motor and physiological manifestations	Open	It is one that is accompanied by motor responses.	Turning the head when perceiving a loud sound
	Covert	No discernible response	Trying to listen in on a conversation without the protagonists noticing it
Subject interest	Divided	Refers to that which is captured by several modules simultaneously.	someone is working on the computer and listening to music.
	Selective	It occurs when the individual focuses his or her interest on a single stimulus, even though the environment may vary from one stimulus to another.	Talking to only one person when at a party
Sensory mode	Visual/spatial	Depends on the sensory capacity to which it is applied y is related to space	Examples are watching a peKcula and listening to the radio, respectively.
	Auditory/temporal	Depends on the sensory capacity to which it is applied y is related to the length of time the stimulus lasts	

Note. Own creation taken from (UNID, 2010).

These types of attention, as mentioned by (UNID, 2010), are determined in each action that describe the criteria of the children, and are fundamental to be able to define the attention deficit in each case and in each context, so that depending on the activity to be developed, it will be possible to measure what type of stimulus generates the attentional process in the child and will provide fundamental bases for the approach to the investigation according to the particular and general needs of the school context.

In the school environment, it is fundamental that the child takes ownership of the attentional processes in all the interactions that they generate in their social and cultural environment.

and outside the classroom, understanding education from the development of cognitive capacities of the subject as an articulator of the experiential processes in contexts complementary to the school, and in the understanding of the elements of the environment with the purpose of generating stable brain connections within the learning processes, establishing the importance of attentional processes in this work, as well as perception and memory, areas that must work hand in hand for educational quality, performance and social accommodation that all these elements provide (Ocampo, 2011).

Technological Mediations

New scenarios for the mediated development of ICT are established in various sectors of modern society and, of course, in the educational field, new strategies are being generated every time to dynamise the teaching and learning processes, processes that have a structure within the pedagogical transformations of each context, thus, different trends emerge that "alter" the academic processes to support their construction, execution and feedback, articulating face-to-face and virtual processes, opting to dynamise the classroom or the academic space in an innovative way (Munoz, 2016).

As Cristobal Cobo expresses it, "The binomial children and technology is so sweet that even the most sceptical", hence the fundamental impact of industries around the world that focus their efforts on generating content for this type of population, given that the new trends in education contain a large accumulation of technological mediations, in relation to the above (Cobo, 2016) establishes a triangulation of interesting vectors to define the importance of each type within the process of teaching and learning mediated with technologies, On the one hand, he establishes *content* as everything that is the raw material of a curricular programme, challenging the teacher to have a specific analysis of the information in order to be able to connect said content with a large number of sources that are provided by means of technologies, The second point is the container, which is based on the support that stores, transports, exchanges, modifies and distributes the contents depending on a relationship in different directions which facilitates the apprehension of the contents and finally the context which refers to the set of physical and symbolic circumstances that establish a certain way of processing knowledge, and this last one can favour or disfavour the whole learning process or the programme in which the students have been linked to. In summary, these three aspects are fundamental and play an ideal role in creating, executing and evaluating an educational process mediated with technologies from the point of view of the attention processes of children at an early age.

Until this very morning, a teacher, in his classroom or in the amphitheatre, delivered a knowledge that was already partly in the books", "The centred or focussed space of the classroom or the amphitheatre can also be drawn as the volume of a vehicle, a train, a car, an aeroplane, in which the passengers, seated in rows in the carriage, the passenger compartment or the fuselage, allow themselves to be driven by the one who guides them towards knowledge" (Serres): train, car, plane, in which the passengers, seated in rows in the carriage, the passenger compartment or the fuselage, allow themselves to be led by the one who guides them towards knowledge" (Serres, 2014), Phrases taken from the book Thumbelina that make us reflect on the changes that are developing rapidly with the appearance of new technologies and the changes that must be carried out in the activities of all educational contexts in order to strengthen them pedagogically, The project is a project of the European Commission to develop a new strategy for the development of the new technologies and the changes that must be carried out in the activities of all the educational contexts to strengthen them pedagogically, to make them more efficient, effective and innovative, questioning the teacher as the only creator of knowledge, so that all the strategies that move around the processes of teaching and learning with the impact and the mediation of the technologies in the classroom or the context of learning of the child and the child can be used as a tool for the development of the new technologies.

The education of children should be guided by the idealistic precepts of a quality education not necessarily linked only to the technological field but articulated between the different means that allow to adjust and understand the educational processes of students in their first years of school life, because the human being must have the possibility to create, think, share their knowledge and use the medications according to the needs without neglecting the autonomy of knowledge (Morales & Rodriguez, 2018).

Gamification

The term began to be popular in mid-2010 when digital environments were incentivised with rewards, understanding that sometimes there are processes that become "boring" within the educational context, and that is where gamification proposes motivational aspects with the aim of achieving recognition and goals that contribute to intellectual development, the removal of barriers, making activities more enjoyable, resulting in individual motivational processes that can be applied in different areas of life (Rodnguez & Raul, 2015). Gamification is not always just creating a game with the aim of having fun, this goes beyond a pedagogical understanding with methodical purposes, for this reason it complies with the characteristics framed by some content creators of google where they state that, to obtain the sustained attention of children, three fundamental points must converge, sound, colour and movement, then, from the applicability to technology, gamification undoubtedly provides essential components for the apprehension of content to improve the attentional processes.

Within the didactics in contemporary educational times in the teaching-learning processes, we see reflected more and more, activities carried out with gamification and structural elements that take elements of the characteristics of the game, to articulate them with the pedagogical processes in different educational contexts, giving a leading role to the actors of the educational process, because the student must have an active participation in the performance of the activities, and of course the teacher proposes its structure to strengthen knowledge and take them out of the conventional standards of education (Oliva, 2016). Not everything that is structured as a game within the educational context should be taken as gamification, so it is important to structure the contents with the appropriate components created to have the right impact within the strategy, and to be able to take full advantage of this wonderful creation used in different educational and training contexts.

Physical Activity

The concept of physical activity is defined as any human movement that generates an important caloric expenditure. Throughout history, human beings have always had physical activity present in all actions that determined their survival and adaptive processes. However, physical activity in children plays a fundamental role in motor and cognitive development, providing health benefits and lifelong habits; during childhood it strengthens the muscular, skeletal and cardiorespiratory systems, and maintains the balance of all physiological processes, reducing the risk of contracting non-communicable diseases during growth, and in cognitive processes it favours socialisation, feelings of personal satisfaction and mental well-being (Aznar & Webster, 2009).

Linking the complementary work processes to physical activity (Crisol & Campos, 2019) proposes the functional motor complements of 6-year-old children with ADHD, which contributes to the articulation of all the processes both at school and in the context of the home, and the impact that the physical activity actions proposed in this research will have with the support of the other stimuli carried out.

- Stimulating control:

- Seat the student close to the tutor and away from windows to avoid distractions.

- Maintain physical and visual contact to attract their attention. - Place him next to the quietest and hardest-working colleagues.

- Improve autonomy:

- Alternate time for work, play and rest. - Adapt tasks to their attention span.

- Assign responsibilities.

- Reward him/her when he/she is attentive. - Work at an individual table for more concentrated activities.

- **Establish daily routines:** daily assembly, relaxation and concentration exercises at the beginning of the task, timetables with drawings that reflect what is going to be done at each moment of the morning, an assembly at the end of the day to review everything that has been worked on...etc.

- **Organisation and planning:** Rehabilitation of executive functions in 6-year-old children with ADHD.

- Divide activities into small tasks.

- Reward the child every time he/she performs an activity without being distracted.

- Putting a headset on for work can help to avoid distractions.

- Realisation of colourful and entertaining activities.

- Clear, simple and precise rules.

- Ask questions to make sure you understand.

- Class leader.

In relation to the most effective treatment for the control of ADHD, it is mentioned (Loro, et al., 2009) that it should be a purely individual intervention with a multimodal character combining in many cases the i'armacologfa with psychosocial behavioural interventions, however more recent research establishes the importance of physical activity in brain processes with benefits in the control of the symptoms of the disorder, and as a coadjuvant with other treatments, because physical activity helps to improve cognitive processes and in mental health generates a balance that enhances educational processes, for example aerobic exercise with moderate intensity iniluencia inhibitory controls contributing in the attentional processes in the school environment (Carriedo, 2014). The environment where the child interacts with the disorder should be ideal to generate bonds of friendship and hobbies that always generate an optimal mood, and when we talk about the school that favourable space belongs primarily to the physical education classes where the teacher must be committed to the educational processes with dynamic, organised, pleasant and always supervised classes to generate the impact that is required in children, these environments when developed in a timely and planned manner have quite good results.

The child with signs of the disorder has a favourable impact on the development of all the contexts in which he or she develops and affects all the physiological and cognitive processes required to ensure that the control of the symptoms does not affect his or her adolescence and adulthood.

Motor and Cognitive Development

Cognitive development is closely linked to motor stimulation and development, taking into account that through movement neural networks are generated that allow different cognitive patterns to be conceived and how to develop in different spaces not only for learning but also for social, family and sporting activities, among other positive actions that contribute to a more integrated performance, impacting the educational context. We define cognitive development by taking some concepts proposed by Piaget and Vygotsky which for the purposes mediated with technologies bring us some interesting guidelines within this process, Piaget on his side manifested his individuality in learning that then articulates with the contexts, which leads to the need to address children with ADHD signs in a particular way according to their characteristics, and on the other hand Vygotsky, who in turn stated that social interaction helped the child to acquire their learning in a more effective way and we relate it to the social impact in good environments that must be guaranteed to the child with the disorder so that they can develop affectively within any context throughout their development (Tomas & Almenara, 2008). Almenara, 2008).

For its part, the motor component is linked to the physiological component and its global physical maturation of its systems, and the achievements become evident each time the child achieves a mastery of the body and the environment, which in turn generates better social relations and fundamental links for the full development of the children and sometimes impacting their academic processes. In effect the motor and cognitive processes have a very close relationship within the development of the children and the concept of psychomotricity appears which alternates and articulates the two processes to generate appropriation and apprehension in the interactions that the child has with the internal and external stimuli to strengthen and improve more and more their cognitive and motor processes, being fundamental to approach the strategy taking into account the particularity of each case with the psychomotor actions that must be executed to strengthen their attentional processes within any context, but clearly approaching it from the educational (Maganto & Cruz, 2018). Cruz, 2018).

The inadequate psychomotor development can generate difficulties in learning as educational contexts require certain attentional and self-regulation conditions that sometimes children with the disorder are unable to adapt and therefore dropout or repetition appear as shown by studies in some European countries in which formality, the execution of complex activities and the organisation of activities make the pedagogical process even more difficult, not reaching the same academic achievements (Suarez, 2017); movement is fundamental for acquiring and perfecting all the child's functions, language, reading, writing and speaking begin with motor processes, allowing interaction with the different environments according to the needs of each case, providing mind-body relationships and adaptability in the field that is needed (Hergueras, 2016), which is why it is so important to find an immediate approach to the impact of the disorder in the educational field so that the child has an intellectual capacity that is at least equal to the rest, it will be difficult for them to achieve their academic achievements due to the lack of attention or regulation respectively in terms of their particularity of symptoms in the disorder and its interaction with the determined contexts (Estevez, 2015), in summary, an approach is required in all areas where the child develops in order to obtain control of the motor and cognitive processes and lead them to a development as "normal" as possible through activities that will impact their psychomotor skills and their social, family and educational interactions.

3 Regulatory Framework

In the relationship of rights that a child with special needs has as a Colombian citizen in the social and educational fields, there are sections of coverage and relevance that advocate for the optimal conditions for him/her to develop in the best way, and to be able to strengthen his/her processes as he/she grows and to guarantee that he/she is an independent human being and apt to be part of society. For the aforementioned reasons, the law 1098 of 2006, which in its article 1 prioritises equality, human dignity in favour of the family and social development of children without any discrimination for their condition or different capacities; in its articles 28 and 29 defines the right to a quality education in early childhood, establishing emotional, cognitive and social bases respecting their rights.

The public policy of Law 1804 of 2016 articulates the principles set out in the Constitution, the Code of Childhood and Adolescence and national and international legislation associated with protecting the mechanisms of action and participation of children in Colombia; The integral development is expressed within the particularity of each child contemplated from 0 to 6 years of age, in which the significant considerations that strengthen the capacities and in itself all the necessary components to promote habits that are required for the entire life cycle starting with early childhood are manifested. In article 4, section e, the national tool is managed to attend to the particular needs in an articulated manner between the state entities, delegating functions for all the programmes that are developed from this initiative, such as the integrated care route (RIA).

Compiling the considerations that govern the educational system in Colombia, and considering the aims of the investigation, in chapter 5, article 69, general parameters of action are defined in relation to the methods and contents suitable for each particular context, seeing it as a process of inclusion within the educational system, facilitating that any Colombian can appropriate the social and educational aspect in their free development of public learning with programmes and processes according to the general and particular needs of the population, favouring the integral development framed by this law, regardless of context, socio-economic stratum, capacities of the child or simply an adaptation of those who require social or educational rehabilitation, this understood as adjustments in the individualised academic processes.

Decree 1421 of 2017 is the governing body of inclusive education which emanates the schematic route and the conditions of the population with special needs, in the educational context, in order to achieve quality, relevance, equity, interculturality, diversity and participation of children covered by the state's education systems. The access and coupling of the educational processes are defined as inclusive within the particular contexts, being flexible and adaptable to strengthen the ways in which the need is latent and is a guarantor of human development well conditioned by the appropriate academic support, attending to the different characteristics, possibilities, interests.

The PIAR (Individual Plan for Reasonable Adjustment) is designed to support the process by providing support for the individual and social needs of the population in pleasant, well-designed environments, favouring human rights and adjusting the relevant aspects of their educational process. As a support to the process, the PIAR (Individual Plan of Reasonable Adjustments) article 2.3.3.5.I.4. numeral 11, of this pedagogical and social assessment is designed, which includes support and reasonable adjustments to guarantee the teaching and learning process, as an input of institutional documents.

4 Methodological Framework

Approach

This research is focused under a mixed approach framed in a work of social character where they intervene with the corresponding analyses to give reliability to the investigation, in this case the methods converge starting sequentially with the qualitative phase and ending with the quantitative phase, as a strategy of articulation (Lopez & fachelli, 2015), this approach will provide a planned design in the creation and evaluation of a pedagogical platform, structured, as a fundamental input in the work and under the indicated parameters guaranteeing the improvement of the attentional processes in children with signs of ADHD. Being of mixed character the process of social investigation determines a plurality of methodologies that will work as guarantors of the possibility of favouring the methodological perspectives so that in this case the processes are strengthened according to the needs of each boy and girl.

Working under a mixed approach favours the dynamics of working with the community and the reliability of the data collected, integrating all the contexts where the children develop, favouring through basic physical exercises and other activities a positive impact on some neuronal processes throughout human development in the first years of life.

The structure of the platform forges a qualifiable and evaluable process within the research, by allowing to measure each of the 5 stages in a structured way with the purpose of generating a professional argumentation of the content articulating the attentional components with the ICT support and harmonising the purposes of the research with the applicability in the specific field of action, all the above supported by pre and post evaluations of the process, guaranteeing a comparative scale of the impact of the process on the participating children.

Design

The process is supported with daily actions framed in the usual context of the child, that is to say that they are participants in their problem, it will be supported in the conceptual paths of the research-action design, in first measure it is intended to design and apply an effective virtual learning environment, to impact from a social educational context to a population with attentional deficiencies of ADHD, so that from there a process of support of the population can be gestated in order to collate the available data of each case and solve a daily problem.

The attentional pedagogical strategy analyses the theoretical and experiential contents of the population, as a support to the academic arguments that contribute to the implementation of the evaluation process, supported by a technological platform that works as an instrument in the execution and interaction with the study population, with the aim of

generate the improvements that indicate an articulation of the appropriate mechanisms to attend the attentional difficulties as framed in the process, the design is taken taking into account the concrete approach to the problem, adjusting to the needs of the individuals and contributing within the processual event of neurological, social, educational development, and in general of all the events in which the attentional processes are interacting (Salgado, 2007), supported by the tool as mediation and in its components.

Outreach

The research will have an exploratory scope, by determining the monitoring and possible control of an unspecified social phenomenon and its main properties according to the immediate context (Hernandez, Fernnandez, & Baptista, 1991), approaching the proposal from a different perspective by approaching a novel context such as the use of digital tools within the everyday context, using simple and intuitive activities mediated by technoiography and new pedagogical processes.By having this scope, the research includes a very inherent responsibility to the personal results and their long-term social impact that will determine a path for future studies or approaches within the attentional process of children with Attention Deficit Hyperactivity Disorder (ADHD). It focuses on a framework that has been little explored as there is no pedagogical strategy that addresses the attentional difficulties in the population with signs of ADHD and that structures a binding process where children can develop planned and articulated activities with the aim of contributing to their educational development and at the same time impacting other contexts where the child develops.

Population

The research project will be conceived as a social proposal with the rigorousness that this requires, in the homogeneity of the population the process will be carried out with boys and girls of the IED Bravo Paez of ages between 7 and 8 years, of socioeconomic strata 1, 2 and 3, the time in which the complete proposal is developed is one month of articulated work and 2 months of planning and filling in documents concerning permits, informed consents and various requirements, The space in which we will work will be virtual by means of digital platforms all mediated by a VLE (virtual learning environment) which will guide all the activity and the process during the stipulated time of planning, execution and evaluation, and finally work with 10 students of the cycle and the characteristics mentioned, characterizing the population suitable for the research process from all phases (Hernandez S. , 2013).

The final analysis took into account the articulation of the digital contents with the population, given as validated by an interdisciplinary team that will allow to approve the reliability of the ATENTI pedagogical strategy.

Data Collection Instruments

For this project, two processes were carried out in which different instruments were used.

Validation of the platform

The survey is, according to (Hueso & Cascant, 2012) being structured and allowing questions of different levels, allows the collection of data and information within a specific scheme of investigation, and for the precise case of the validation of the virtual learning environment, two structured surveys were generated to validate the relevance of the contents and the means of implementation of the space, the first one addressed to professional experts in the development of virtual learning environments, which verify the organisation, comprehension and functionality of all the elements of the VLE, which would make an intuitive and pleasant experience to the claims of the attentional pedagogical strategy, and the second one addressed to professional experts in the development of virtual learning environments, which verify the organisation, comprehension and functionality of all the elements of the VLE, which would make an intuitive and pleasant experience to the claims of the attentional pedagogical strategy, and functionality of all the elements of the AVA, which made an intuitive and pleasant experience to the pretensions of the attentional pedagogical strategy, and the second one directed to professional experts psychologists, who verify the exercises and activities of the whole proposal, with the purpose that they fulfil the requirements proposed in the objectives of study and really contribute to that attentional improvement in the different contexts but impacted mainly in the educational environment.

Pretest and posttest

Validating the possibility of achieving an improvement in the attentional processes of the participating children by means of the attentional pedagogical strategy ATENTI, two validated tests are taken which for the relevant purposes are the most suitable to compare the process in a before or pre-process conceived with the child when making the initial contact and an after or post process which is located at the end of all the virtual activities; these tests were implemented by competent professionals by means of the Mempas platform.

Tracking test -TMT

It consists of performing a sequence of numbers and letters in the shortest possible time, it is divided into two parts, part a: numbers, part b: numbers and letters, this test explores selective and divided attention, and other components that shed light on a deeper work in the behavioural aspects of children such as tolerance to frustration, focus, sequencing, executive functions, impulsivity, among others. For the development, the protocols established for its implementation were followed, in terms of times, sequences and follow-ups.

- Colour and word test-STROOP

It consists of presenting sheets with colours and words, where the participant must achieve the sequence of reading words, identification of colour with interference, the test explores selective, divided, focused attention, perception, processing speed, which in an educational environment provides tools for monitoring behavioural processes and the acquisition of new knowledge. It has been validated for more than 80 years as an effective tool for evaluating psychopathological effects in the study population, used in different ways according to the needs of the evaluator or researcher, contributing on this occasion in the context of experimental research (Ruiz, Luque, & Sanchez, 2020).

Risks covered by the investigation

No risks associated with the research are contemplated, since the entire process has the consent of the population, validators and experts, and the times for each of the processes or stages of the research are calculated. In addition, the resources

The research does not require special permissions or licences of use that would prevent the progress and successful completion of the processes of the pedagogical strategy, and finally, as it is a product of its own creation, there are no conflicts with entities, organisations or natural persons that would prevent the execution of the research proposal.

Measures to Deal with Complications

Due to the atypical situation of the research proposal, complications were minimised to the maximum, firstly the validation structure of experts committed to the process and who will contribute their professional knowledge to ensure that the ATENTI pedagogical strategy has all the requirements and optimal parameters to have a positive impact on the lives of the children who will be involved later on, Secondly, the tests are mechanisms that have been validated by experts and are undoubtedly suitable for verifying the premises of the evaluation process. Virtuality is the number one ally in this process, since, as previously mentioned, the pandemic has not allowed for face-to-face meetings, but this was not an impediment to completing the process.

5 Analysis of Results

For the analysis of the results, an articulation is made between the response of the expert, comparison with related authors and finally the opinion of the creators on two types of surveys supported under the Questionpro platform, one from a pedagogical perspective validated by two professionals in psychology, who evaluate the relevance of the activities and the concordance of the processes, and another on the digital perspective, validating the virtual learning environment, in its form, accessibility and functionality. For the field work in the execution of the process, a time of 4 weeks was established, applying 5 activities per week, that is to say one activity per week from Monday to Friday, with entrance tests and then comparative tests at the end of the process, with which the relevance of the platform and the impact of the strategy on the participating children were measured.

Platform Design

The process of the research was developed under a virtual learning environment, which will be supported on the WIX platform with the link https://waltermurillosierr.wixsite.com/atenti, this environment will have a very striking and relevant design for the work, within its structure it will have five modules or work sessions distributed as follows:

Activity 1: the first activity starts with a physical activation supported on the youtube platform that lasts approximately 3 minutes, in which the children will perform functional motor exercises; Activity 2: in the second activity called "atentiactivity", a template is created that favours the different types of attention and visual tracking, favouring cognitive stimuli; Activity 3: In this activity, movement exercises are combined with the use of specific attention schemes; Activity 4: This activity focuses on gamification, where in each session the children will have a challenge mapped out by means of a game, supported by the Genially platform; Activity 5: In each session, participants will fill in a form where they will provide their perceptions of each session.

The activities are designed to be developed in sessions of maximum 25 minutes, or according to each process. The idea is to structure a pedagogical strategy focused on strengthening the attentional processes of children through a platform that is easy to use, eye-catching and that articulates the general contents with the applicability of each context, and as an additional positive point of the process is the adhesion of links between parents and their children, since this topic is fundamental to culminate and to obtain the impact desired by the creators of ATENTI.

The virtual learning environment has 6 tabs of related links within the tool, each space is designed with a purpose that orders the process of the pedagogical strategy, providing the user with an intuitive experience.

• **In** the first part of the VPA the main information related to the objective, purpose, and description of the strategy is established, there are virtual support links with easy to use tools that will provide more content and activities, as well as the explanation of each of the sessions (see annex a).

• **Pestana 2 Information for parents:** This space frames all the relevant information about ADHD and other links of interest related to the processes of attention of children, it is aimed at parents or guardians who accompany the process (see annex b).

• This material can be downloaded in PDF format ready to be printed or to be used on the net, there you can find material not only for the daily activities, but also support booklets for autonomous activities in the family (see annex c).

• **Tab 4 Activities:** In this tab you will find the links for each of the sessions, clicking on it opens a PDF file containing the 5 activities of the session, each activity is developed in a support platform that is directly addressed by clicking on the hyperlink (see appendix d).

• **Pestana 5 Contact:** In this pestana you can find the data of the creators, as well as leave a message with the personal data to contact the user via e-mail (see annex e).

• **Panel 6 Registration or login:** In order to ensure privacy and security of the session, in this part of the VPA, the user is allowed to register with an email address and then log in to access all the content of the strategy in a secure way (see annex f).

Pretest and posttest

For the detection and clinical diagnosis of ADHD, it is evaluated from the integral aspect of the quantitative with standardised tests and performance tests to specify conditions, effects, and characteristics of the individual and in the qualitative by means of observation of the context and the real behaviour of the child in conventional aspects of daily development (Aidyne, 2018), these two aspects are articulated in order to provide an objective report on the conditions of each case. Although to evaluate attention is not only done to perceive effects associated with the disorder and as stated by (Rodnguez M., 2014) there are countless tests, understanding that attention is not unitary and is perceived from different components that focus it and take it to different positions of study and is associated with independent brain actions according to each action, and that is why the tests are delimited by each claim of investigative work.

For the specific intervention process in cases of ADHD detected or under study, the educational field plays a fundamental role in being able to collate and compile all the information about the strong aspects or those to be improved and if there are associated academic difficulties in order to generate the work and intervention plan for the child; the interdisciplinary team undoubtedly supports all the necessary actions in the intervention process and the educational field as an agent of this interdisciplinary team ensures comprehensive development (see figure 10), and from there strengthens processes that are reflected in the different contexts in which the children develop (Balbuena, et al., 2014).

Figure 1 *Process of detection, evaluation and intervention with ADHD students*

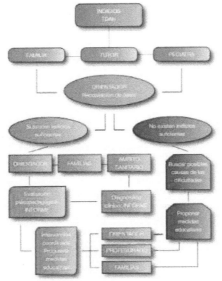

From the above it can be inferred that the research focused on the tests that made it possible to measure the attentional difficulties linked to Attention Deficit and Hyperactivity Disorder, and from there to contribute to the process of the attentional pedagogical strategy in order to generate a comparison and evaluate whether there is an associated impact; The first test used was the tracking test -TMT, in which two tests were carried out, in test A the tracking of only numbers in sequence from 1 located in different spaces of the test was followed, for test B the tracking of numbers and letters in sequence was carried out, where number and letter are alternated respectively, at the end the time taken by the boy or girl in each of the tests was taken; the second test used was STROPP test of

23

colours and words, in which the updated scales were used.

"The STROOP is composed of three different tasks or conditions. In the **task 1**, also called condition P word or condition P, is a sheet with the words "RED", "GREEN" and "BLUE" in random order and printed in black ink. The same word never appears twice consecutively in the same column. The task is for the test taker to read aloud the words that are written. In **task 2**, also called condition Colour or condition C, a sheet is presented with a series of sets of four x's ("XXXX") printed in blue, green or red ink. The same colour does not appear twice consecutively in the same column, nor does it correspond to the order of the words on the sheet in task 1. In this condition, the respondent's task is to name the colour of the ink in which the "X "s are printed. In task 3, also called the Word-Colour condition or PC condition, a slide is presented in which the same words from the slide in task 1 appear, but printed in the same colours as the sets of Xs in task 2. That is, element 1 of **task 3** is the word that appears as element 1 of task 1 (RED) but printed in the ink of the colour of element 1 of task 2 (blue ink). In this way, the colour of the ink never matches the name of the written colour and there is always incongruence between the word and the colour of the ink. In this condition the task of the tested person is to name the colour of the ink in which each word is printed. A time limit of 45 seconds is provided for each task. The complete application of the test, including the instructions, requires approximately 5 minutes" (Ruiz, Luque, & Sanchez, 2020).

Pretest

Table 3 *Pretest*

N°	Genre	Age	Grade	Test Entry						
				TMT tracking		STROOP				
				A	B	P	C	PC		R-Int
1	Nina 1	7 years	Second	25	50	15	16	6	7,74194	-1,74193548
2	Nina2	7 years	Second	34	49	14	15	5	7,24138	-2,24137931
3	Nino3	8 years	Second	25	60	13	14	6	6,74074	-0,74074074
4	Nino4	7 years	Second	22	62	15	13	7	6,96429	0,03571429
5	Nino5	7 years	Second	30	58	12	15	8	6,66667	1,33333333
6	Nina6	8 years	Second	24	50	14	12	5	6,46154	-1,46153846
7	Nino 7	7 years	Second	22	53	16	16	6	8	-2
8	Nina8	7 years	First	29	65	12	13	8	6,24	1,76
9	Nina9	8 years	Second	27	57	13	15	4	6,96429	-2,96428571
10	Nino 10	7 years	Second	26	70	11	16	5	6,51852	-1,51851852

Note: The table shows the results of the children's entry tests.

participants.

In the application of the entrance tests, some variances are evident with respect to the international scales that are established to measure the attentional deficit, the data obtained were fundamental to perceive the support and suitable pedagogical planning that was given to the ATENTI activities, TMT Tracking Test:

According to the results obtained in the pretest, the attentional deficit of the children is framed in the difficulty of presentation of the test, by evidencing the lack of association and logical sequencing of numbers and letters, which in consideration is established as a work process within the tests that were developed in the strategy, focusing some of the activities on sequencing work, focusing, psychomotor processing speed, selective and divided attention. When focusing and executing determining actions to measure attention, some aspects that may be interfering in the daily processes, among them the educational process, are evidenced, and from there efforts were focused on imparting general actions to define at the end of the process the relevance of the attentional pedagogical strategy.

For the educational environment, selective attention provides the necessary patterns so that the child can choose to focus on the relevant information of a given process, and on the contrary, irrelevant information can move to the "background", so that the response can be even more effective

(Ballesteros, 2014), and to be able to determine in each action the articulation with other neural impulses, improving the complementary processes throughout the life cycle, since the importance of these approaches in attention underpin the purpose of the research, the process was adapted to the results obtained.

Stropp Test

Inhibitory attentional control facilitates the suppression of unnecessary or unusual actions, with the aim of attending to tasks in a more conscious manner with more precise results and preparing the system for increasingly complex activities that require a more detailed work of the brain processes, according to the results obtained, in the first and third task there is evidence of a difficulty in differentiating the purposes of the test, that is to say that the parameters for involving divided attention also gained importance within the planning of the activities of the attentional pedagogical strategy.

In this process, divided attention, which is understood as the capacity to carry out two or more tasks with the necessary requirements to carry them out without truncating the actions or resources available depending on the difficulty involved, can also be indispensable for some of the children's academic actions. In particular, it is based on the attentional deficiency that frames the test and on the actions that were taken to strengthen this attentional process according to the necessary articulation to improve the general attentional processes impacted in the daily contexts of the participating children.

Execution of working sessions

In the first step, 20 individual work sessions were developed through the virtual learning environment, which were focused on the necessary "pre-improvements" and abstracted from the initial tests, these activities varied in their purposes and levels of difficulty according to the progress of the process.

In the first agreement made with each of the guardians, the item of commitment in the attendance and execution of the activities was fundamental in the autonomous virtual meetings in the virtual learning environment AVA, where a percentage of total participation of over 90% was evident (see table 4), which shows a reliability in the final data collected by means of the comparative tests in each case, in addition, the

participation guarantees to obtain data on the easiest and most complex activities, which individually provides a comparative scale of activities that can be left as academic recommendations.

Table *4Total* **participation** *in activities*

N°	Genre	Age	Grade	Participation in daily activities																				Total Part
				Week 1					Week 2					Week 3					Week 4					
				1	2	3	4	5	6	7	8	9	10	11	12	13	14	15	16	17	18	19	20	
1	Nina 1	7 years	Second	1	1	1	1	1	1	1	1	1	1	1	1	1	1	1	1	1	1	1	1	20
2	Nina 2	7 years	Second	1	1	1	1	1	1	1	1	1	1	1	1	1	1	1	1	1	1		1	19
3	Nino 3	8 years	Second	1	1	1	1	1	1	1	1	1	1	1	1	1	1	1	1	1	1	1		19
4	Nino 4	7 years	Second	1					1	1	1	1	1	1	1	1	1	1	1	1	1	1	1	18
5	Nino 5	7 years	Second	1	1	1	1	1	1	1	1		1	1	1	1	1	1	1	1	1	1	1	19
6	Nina 6	8 years	Second	1	1	1	1	1	1	1	1	1	1	1	1	1	1	1	1	1	1	1	1	20
7	Nino 7	7 years	Second	1	1	1	1	1	1	1	1		1	1	1	1	1	1	1	1	1	1	1	19
8	Nina 8	7 years	First	1	1	1	1	1	1	1	1	1	1	1	1	1	1	1	1	1	1	1	1	20
9	Nina 9	8 years	Second	1	1			1	1	1	1	1	1	1	1	1	1	1	1	1	1	1	1	18
10	Nino 10	7 years	Second	1	1	1	1	1	1	1	1	1	1	1	1	1	1	1	1	1	1	1	1	20
																								192

Improving the attentional conditions and therefore some motor aspects of the children is the fundamental objective of the research, and it is there, when it is reviewed in each of the sessions which activities were developed more quickly and easily (see table 5), which leads to deduce which form of attentional work is more assertive for the process of subsequent recommendations, it is thus as evidenced in the results obtained that the activities that retain some scheme of motor work had the greatest ease and the best execution time, which contrasts with (Marchan & Mera, 2020), who link the deficit of motor development to children diagnosed with or with signs of ADHD, this because, due to their condition, they are prone to poor development of basic skills, loss of basic skills, loss of motor development, etc.), which is due to the fact that, due to their condition, they are prone to the poor development of basic skills, loss of motor development and the lack of motor development. Mera,

2020), who link the deficit in motor development to children diagnosed with ADHD or with signs of ADHD, due to the fact that because of their condition they are prone to poor development of basic skills, loss of balance, coordination, due to internal or external situations; although the activities conserve basic movement schemes, it can be inferred that the motor aspect motivates the attentional adaptation in the different spectrums of the work.

Motor development is fundamental in almost all daily processes, and it is there where this development is articulated with the processes that should favour the different types of attention in children. However, it should be noted that the comparative is much more precise when the results of the more complex activities and those that took longer to develop are indicated, as this will determine a working path in the conclusions.

Table 5*Activities carried out more easily and in less time*

Activity carried out more easily

N°	Genre	Age	Grade	Week 1					Week 2					Week 3					Week 4					Predom
				1	2	3	4	5	6	7	8	9	10	11	12	13	14	15	16	17	18	19	20	
1	Nina 1	7 years	Second	1	1	1	1	1	1	4	4	1	1	1	4	1	1	4	1	1	1	4	4	1
2	Nina 2	7 years	Second	1	4	1	4	4	1	4	4	1	4	4	1	4	4	1	1	1	4		4	4
3	Nino 3	8 years	Second	1	1	3	3	1	3	3	3	3	3	1	1	3	1	1	3	3	1	1		3
4	Nino 4	7 years	Second	4		4	4	1	4	1		4	1	1	4	4	1	1	4	4	1	4	1	4
5	Nino 5	7 years	Second	1	1	1	1	1	1	1	1	1		1	1	1	1	1	1	1	1	1	1	1
6	Nina 6	8 years	Second	1	1	1	1	1	1	1	1	1	1	1	1	1	1	1	1	1	1	1	1	1
7	Nino 7	7 years	Second	1	4	1	4	1	1	4	1		1	1	4	3	4	1	1	4	3	4	1	1
8	Nina 8	7 years	Prime ro	4	4	4	4	4	4	4	4	4	4	4	4	4	4	4	4	4	4	4	4	4
9	Nina9	8 years	Second	1	4		3	1	1	3		3	1	3	4	1	4	1	3	3	1	3	2	1-3
10	Nino 10	7 years	Second	1	1	1	1	4	1	1	1	1	4	1	1	1	1	4	1	1	1	1	4	1

More complex tasks or tasks with a higher attentional need tend to worsen social conditions, and among them the academic aspect is impacted as children sometimes find themselves in situations of isolation, In effect, the results of the activity that caused the most difficulty and time in execution (see table 6), were undoubtedly the activities where the child needed a more complex sequence of steps to focus and execute an action, without the need for a more complex approach.

However, (Flores, 2016) states that it should be taken into account that children in early developmental stages are distracted by the slightest stimulus, without being able to manage the different types of attention in a voluntary manner, adducing this dispersed condition to multiple social and family factors which does not always become a pathological factor, and ultimately, this argument further approves the need for increasingly accurate diagnoses to be able to work from the correct perspective the attentional deficit. In the case of children with clinical indications or diagnoses, the strategy undoubtedly strengthens the attentional processes from different perspectives, acting with the moments, stimuli and virtual scenarios necessary to enhance their attentional capacities and, incidentally, the academic processes that underlie the daily stimuli.

Table 6 *Most difficult and time-consuming activities to carry out*

N°	Genre	Age	Grade	Activity developed with greater difficulty																				Total Part
				Week 1					Week 2					Week 3					Week 4					
				1	2	3	4	5	6	7	8	9	10	11	12	13	14	15	16	17	18	19	20	
1	Nina 1	7 years	Second	2	2	2	2	2	2	2	2	2	2	2	2	2	2	2	2	2	2	2	2	2
2	Nina 2	7 years	Second	2	2	2	3	2	3	2	3	3	2	2	2	2	2	2	2	2	3		2	2
3	Nino 3	8 years	Second	2	2	2	2	4	2	2	2	2	2	4	2	2	2	4	2	2	2	2		2
4	Nino 4	7 years	Second	2		2	2	2	2	2		2	2	2	2	2	2	2	2	2	2	2	2	2
5	NinoS	7 years	Second	2	3	2	3	3	2	3	3		3	2	3	2	3	2	3	3	3	3	2	3
6	Nina 6	8 years	Second	2	2	2	2	2	2	2		2	2	2	2	2	2	2	2	2	2	2	2	2
7	Nino 7	7 years	Second	3	3	3	3	3	3	3	3		3	3	3	3	3	3	3	3	3	3	3	3
8	Nina 8	7 years	Prime ro	2	3	2	3	2	3	3	2	2	2	2	2	2	2	2	2	2	2	2	2	2
9	Nina9	8 years	Second	2	2		2	2	2	2		2	2	2	2	2	2	2	2	2	2	2	2	2
10	Nino 10	7 years	Second	3	2	3	2	3	2	3	2	2	2	3	2	2	3	3	2	3	2	2	2	2

Posttest

Table 7*Post-test*

N°	Genre	Age	Grade	Test Exit	
				TMT tracking	STROOP

				A	B	P	C	PC	tPC"	R-Int
1	Nina 1	7 years	Second	20	45	17	17	7	8,5	-1,5
2	Nina2	7 years	Second	25	45	15	15	7	7,5	-0,5
3	Nino3	8 years	Second	22	56	16	14	8	7,46667	0,53333333
4	Nino4	7 years	Second	18	55	18	16	10	8,47059	1,52941176
5	Nino5	7 years	Second	25	54	14	16	7	7,46667	-0,46666667
6	Nina6	8 years	Second	23	46	15	13	6	6,96429	-0,96428571
7	Nino 7	7 years	Second	23	50	16	15	7	7,74194	-0,74193548
8	Nina8	7 years	First	25	55	16	17	12	8,24242	3,75757576
9	Nina9	8 years	Second	25	50	14	16	7	7,46667	-0,46666667
10	Nino 10	7 years	Second	25	65	15	15	5	7,5	-2,5

Note: The table shows the results of the children's exit tests.

participants.

Once the work process with the participating children was completed, the exit tests or post-tests were carried out, which gave an objective comparative relation about the process and the viability of the ATENTI attentional pedagogical strategy; (Garces & Suarez, 2014) mentions neuroplasticity as a process that can occur at any stage of human development, where the brain has the capacity to adapt to consecutive stimuli and physiologically reorganises itself according to the physiological reorganisation of the brain. Suarez, 2014) mentions neuroplasticity as a process that can occur at any stage of human development, where the brain has the ability to adapt to consecutive stimuli and physiologically reorganizes according to neuronal reactivity, for this case the stimuli that start from that instructional reinforcement of activities focused on attentional improvements, that give a first step to the activation of the development in the early infantile stage, we speak of this early development in order to link or articulate not only executive processes but also behavioural and voluntary processes according to each need that the daily context poses.

TMT Tracking Test.

In the comparative of the input and output test, a considerable improvement in the comparative processing of the test is evident, that is to say that the execution times decreased in 98% of the participants, speaking of tests A and B, from which it is inferred that the processes of logical sequencing and association improved in some range, impacting the processes of selective and divided attention, as a consequence of the articulated activities where the child had to attend to more than one stimulus and specify the importance of executing adequate functions for each task, in the same way the activities where the child had to use motor skills with differential tasks strengthened the processes of psychomotor processing speed by sharing the need to attend in a divided way in two independent body schemes that in the end are articulated to generate voluntary psychomotor actions.

Cognitive flexibility for the adaptation of new stimuli within the academic process is also strengthened, which greatly favours and makes viable the use of the virtual learning environment as a sequential support for the improvement of the attentional processes in the classroom.

Stropp Test

In this test, improvements in the attentional process were also evident, if we compare the results of the pre-test and post-test, where 99% of the children obtained an improvement in the process, this measured from the capacities of the child in their executive functions, processing speed and divided, selective and focused attention, as is the aim of the standardised stroop test, this as an argument to make the activities that were developed viable, once the results of the first test were known, the activities were focused on strengthening the general conditions of the team to be worked on.

Within the execution and subsequent results of the comparative study, it is demonstrated how the activation of brain areas and their continuous work, guarantees an improvement in any physiological, internal and external environment, which in the long term will guarantee more optimal conditions for those diagnosed with ADHD, achieving behavioural patterns adaptable to any context and a "normal" functionality within everyday life and their conventional life processes, as well as in the educational environment, adapting to the conditions of the "classroom" and their learning of knowledge will be more effective.

Validation by platform experts

For the pedagogical validation of the content and the attentional activities, the link https://www.questionpro.com/t/ARTWDZjVy7 is designated, the form has two parts, the first is a space for personal data and the second, 5 specific questions that validate the pretensions of the research proposal in the pedagogical path.

Figure 2. *Pedagogical validation survey. Part 1.*

Source: own creation.

Pedagogical Validation 1

The first expert, master in psychology and professor at the University of the Andes, who broadens the spectrum of the strategy for the sports field, seeing the relevance of the approach in the initial categories of football.

¿Is there a correspondence between the purpose and the content of the strategy?

First of all, the correspondence between the purpose and the articulated content of ATENTI is determined, since it frames in an organised and simple way each of the contents within the structure designed for each session, starting with a motor stimulation activity that will lead the child to enter a zone of attention.

focused. According to (Caamano, 2018) the processes of metacognition, in which the learning processes are immersed during their development, enable or disable fundamental schemes in capacities or skills that allow different tasks in the academic field and their assimilation within the social and family contexts using techniques and strategies to enhance cognitive processes as in this case, the attentional processes (see figure 2).

Figure 3 Schematic *of metacognitive processes at the academic level*

28

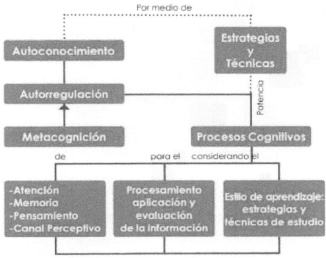

(Caamano, 2018)

reaching an autonomous development of the own skills of concept acquisition.

The ATENTI pedagogical strategy favours the strengthening of the attentional cycle (see figure 3), as a support to the deficit of this process, in short, the contents fully favour the purpose of the attentional activities and the organisation that is given to each session. In each session the purpose is to be able to focus on a type of attention, which links the process within the cognitive development of each activity, that is to say, that each space of interaction allows the adherence of individualised strategies so that the child manages to "overcome" the challenges posed in a calm manner and that guarantees autonomous learning based on metacognitive processes, passing through all the points related to the cycle of attention throughout the process.

Figure 4 *The cycle of care*

(Martrnez, Pacheco, & Nava, 2015) Taken from (Caamano, 2018).

¿Do you consider VPA to be relevant for the attentional approach of children?

A virtual learning environment is ideal to strengthen an attentional approach, as it contains the schemes required to obtain children's attention more easily through the concepts of colours, sounds and movements. Virtual learning environments are facilitating spaces for different ways of teaching, where different functionalities converge, allowing a fluid and active interaction of the actors in the process, leaving aside traditional education as the only source of generating innovative pedagogical experiences when structuring functional pedagogical strategies, in addition, other functions of learning appear such as collaboration between actors and self-knowledge (Cedeno, 2019). In short, virtual learning environments are gaining more and more strength within school environments, by facilitating their structure from any creative environment that leads the user to interact intuitively with the established content.

¿'...Are the theoretical and practical contents articulated in the strategy?

Yes, the contents are articulated, as the VPA is very explanatory in the theoretical concepts and the practical exercises are very clear for their recognition. The pedagogical strategies are actions determined by each creator, which facilitate the structuring and organisation of pedagogical scenarios suitable for the determined contexts, they also define the possibility of transmitting and constructing knowledge if the strategy is well founded and supported with academic rigour and are determined according to the action of the learning scenario (Gamboa, Gartia, & Marlen, 2013). Marlen, 2013), consequently the articulation of the contents is fundamental to give gma of the proposal and in its execution to be able to route the most reliable possible results, then, to take a good theoretical concept will allow that the practical actions are developed more easily within a digital context, allowing the inclusion of any type of population in the pedagogical strategy ATENTI, when making it easy to understand and to execute.

(■ Do you think the strategy is appropriate for the educational context?

Yes, the strategy is very structured for an educational context, but it can also be replicated in the context of sports training, and its contributions are likely to reduce the attentional deficits of boys and girls who start playing football. Sport and physical activity can be an important bridge in the treatment of attention deficit and the acquisition of cognitive skills that favour the normal development of the processes, not only contributes to the socialising processes, but also directs orienting actions such as self-control, discipline, channelling emotions, among other actions that, when articulated with structured processes, provide advantages to these difficulties that are not very positive for their development, on the other hand, there are underlying symptoms of each particularity, and where the processes that are carried out in the different contexts where the children develop are fundamental for their treatment (ADHD, 2012), in other words, the strategy is adapted to the educational context as it was created for this purpose, but its contribution in the sporting environment would ensure that the child has double stimulation, taking advantage of the benefits of each of the contexts and where the benefit will be joint.

('.Additional comments?

None.

The professional triangulation of the first expert concludes the relevance of the ATENTI pedagogical strategy within the educational context, with the purpose of favouring the attentional processes of the children who participate in it, in addition, it is proposed that it can be taken to a sports context, due to the contents related in each session and that, according to the expert, they will improve the processes of sports formation of children who have attentional difficulties. Consequently, the pedagogical strategy is validated in its curricular component, evidencing the pertinence of the contents as activities suitable for executing the strategy in its second phase with the determined population.

Pedagogical validation 2

The second is an expert psychologist from the University of the Andes, a specialist in sports and exercise psychology, who gives a very accurate pedagogical vision of the process.

(■ .is there a correspondence between the purpose and the content of the strategy?

Totally, the content of the strategy is very well thought out; starting with a physiological activation to reach a cognitive activation that will favour the process of attention. A lot of congruence. In the attentional processes, internal and external factors converge, voluntary and involuntary factors that determine the action to develop, or in this case to work on, in particular each activity focuses on a type of attention (see figure 4), hence the exercises are articulated with the necessary congruence to contribute to the different attentional processes, according to each case, and as mentioned (Caamano, 2018) the strategies must be general so that the cognitive process can make them specific according to each need. The correspondence is strategic according to the purposes of each session, and in general of the whole pedagogical strategy, since it is planned according to the activation curve of the children according to their interests, which, due to their age, can influence them quite well.

Figure 5 *Types of care*

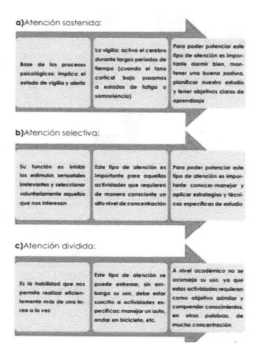

a) Atención sostenida:

Base de los procesos psicológicos: implica el estado de vigilia y alerta	La vigilia: activa el cerebro durante largos periodos de tiempo (cuando el tono cortical bajo pasamos a estados de fatiga o somnolencia)	Para poder potenciar este tipo de atención es importante dormir bien, mantener una buena postura, planificar nuestro estudio y tener objetivos claros de aprendizaje

b) Atención selectiva:

Su función es inhibir los estímulos sensoriales irrelevantes y seleccionar voluntariamente aquellos que nos interesan	Este tipo de atención es importante para aquellas actividades que requieren de manera consciente un alto nivel de concentración	Para poder potenciar este tipo de atención es importante conocer-manejar y aplicar estrategias y técnicas específicas de estudio

c) Atención dividida:

Es la habilidad que nos permite realizar eficientemente más de una tarea a la vez	Este tipo de atención se puede entrenar, sin embargo su uso, debe estar suscrito a actividades específicas: manejar un auto, andar en bicicleta, etc.	A nivel académico no se aconseja su uso, ya que estas actividades requieren como objetivo asimilar y comprender conocimientos, en otras palabras, de mucha concentración

(Caamano, 2018)

(■ Do you consider VPA to be relevant for children's attentional approach?

Virtuality is now more than ever a part of our lives. Platforms such as these promote the virtual learning environment to be used more and more nowadays. The virtual learning environment responds to an instructional design that enhances the operability of each function, around the ease of use, download, view and follow the entire process, so it is an enabling environment that meets the parameters of effectiveness and security that requires a virtual learning environment (Cedeno, 2019). The AVA fulfils an innovative role in the attentional strategy, which at the same time encompasses a series of activities that not only strengthen the attentional processes, but also other characteristics that underlie each work session, topics that should be highlighted as a plus within the pedagogical strategy, which gives more validity to the fact that it is a pedagogical process supported by technology.

¿.are the theoretical and practical contents of the strategy articulated?

Yes, the contents are very well designed, first in each area of the VPA a theoretical concept of what is to be done in practice is presented, in addition at each stage of the process there is a pedagogical identity that allows clarity of the whole strategy. When we talk about articulating theoretical and practical concepts, we must refer in the first place to the didactics designed for this purpose, where we try to link the processes according to the needs and in a way that meets the objectives to be developed within the pedagogical strategy (Alvarez, 2012), and, although sometimes this is a bit complex, for the case of the ATENTI pedagogical strategy, the links are made taking into account the didactic considerations for virtuality and the presentation of virtual learning environments, which in this digital era articulates in the best way the way to make new education and take the technologies by the hand to make the best use of them.

(■ Do you consider the strategy to be appropriate for the educational context?

It is appropriate, as long as time is taken into account. There will be some children who do better than others and it should be promoted that the "competition" is against themselves and in this way a

32

motivational climate oriented to the task and not to the result. This would be a very valuable element in education. All pedagogical strategies are born from a need to provide solution to a certain social situation, and has a certain structure to go through different stages generating knowledge that respond to different sources of solutions, which are finally resolved successfully within the structure, as stated by (Gamboa, Gartia, & Marlen, 2013), where it is stated by (Gamboa, Gartia, & Marlen, 2013), where it is stated by (Gamboa, Gartia, & Marlen, 2013), where it is stated by (Gamboa, Gartia, & Marlen, 2013). Marlen, 2013), where they take a scheme (see figure 5), in which a line is proposed in the construction of knowledge, which in the case of the strategy complies with most of the parameters stipulated in its planning from the pedagogical perspective, then, the strategy from every point of view meets the necessary parameters to be introduced in a pedagogical environment from any educational context.

Figure 6Pathway *to knowledge construction*

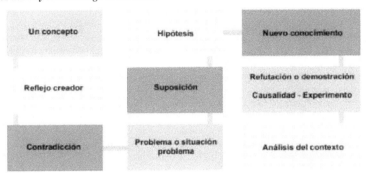

(Gamboa, Gartia, & Marlen, 2013)

('.Additional comments?

The programme is very well thought out and most importantly, it is clear to anyone who accesses it. All the images and activities are downloadable, which makes the exercise even easier.

In conclusion, the strategy is validated from the pedagogical aspect, as it complies with the exposed parameters to obtain a reliability in the implementation of a second phase, considering a fundamental support in the attentional processes, not only in the educational context, but also in possible sports scenarios, demonstrating that the activities are coherent and comply with a curve of mental activation that favours the processes of neuroplasticity, for the age in formation, these processes of adaptation to new stimuli in the nervous system support more complex cognitive processes seen from a perspective of neuronal connections and not of localisation of stimuli (Garces & Suarez, 2014), contributing to the development of the process of neuroplasticity. Suarez, 2014), providing these new spaces of neural connections that allow the child to strengthen adaptive processes within any context, and even more, in contexts that have to do with the pedagogical, where he or she will spend many years of his or her human development, performing activities that will be reflected in his or her adult life. With this knowledge, the strategy is ideal to ensure that a primary approach to ADHD is taken in any context, indicating the necessary steps for an ideal monitoring of children as indicated in studies specialised in the early approach to ADHD.

For the validation of the virtual learning environment, the link https://www.questionpro.com/t/ARTWDZjWU0 is designated, the form has two parts, the first is a space for personal data and the second, 5 specific questions that validate the pretensions of the research proposal in the technological path.

Validation AVA 1

The first expert, an area teacher of the Bogota education secretary, university lecturer and expert in virtual learning environments.

(Is the virtual learning environment intuitive?

The platform offers the possibility of a pedagogical strategy and its tools are in accordance with the purpose of each of the activities.In virtual learning environments, constant support is offered in all stages of the process (planning, execution and evaluation) of teaching and learning, allowing interaction to be forged individually or collectively, individually because activities are carried out specifically for children and collectively because it must involve family and comprehensive support of the process to bring it to a successful conclusion, in addition, that in the collaborative aspect, ideas can be provided, suggestions, which will contribute to everyone in the development of a virtual learning environment (Buzon, 2005), consequently, a virtual learning environment must be intuitive to be inclusive to any context of the population, hence, the ATENTI strategy through its virtual environment, favours its reading and navigability to any person who decides to get involved in its digital content, facilitating the processes to be more receptive for children.

Is the content organised to promote understanding?

The platform is organised by days of the week and their respective additional activities, it has the resources for downloading support guides, images and support videos. Within the concept of the knowledge society that has been incorporated in previous years, the high consumption of technological information, which forces more and more hastily to the creation of new strategies that favour the processes of teaching and learning mediated by technology, at the same time that are structured in an organised way to be navigable in different sources with accurate, truthful information and innovative technological resources that contribute in both directions of the teaching and learning process, and also that link all the actors involved in the process (Vinas, 2018). The virtual learning environment is designed in a very playful way, understanding that the target audience are children of cycle 1 of traditional education, thus, organised contents are generated from each interaction platform, from the explanation of the strategy, to its main content of activities, being a space conducive to the understanding of all its aspects and also providing continuous advice to those who use the virtual learning space.

gIs the VPA user-friendly (navigation, resources, icons, material)?

Simple platform starting with the registration to the page, the video presentation, the downloads of support grnas and images and support videos and the monitoring of activities by days of the week. In order to structure a virtual learning environment that facilitates all actions in navigation, it is necessary to take care of some aspects as mentioned by (Lopez, Ledesma, & Escalera, 2009), one of the most important points is trust, which refers to the guarantee given to the user of the quality of the content, resources and materials used, which ultimately supports a good experience, i.e. downloadable content, space without interruptions and constant support from the creators; the second point is interaction, here, the important thing is that at all times the user has adequate technical and pedagogical support, which resolves their concerns in moderate response times; In the third point, accessibility, care must be taken with the saturation of contents or complementary platforms that are difficult to handle or confusing in the navigation of the virtual environment, in addition the cultural and economic conditions of the participants must be taken into account, to guarantee that it is accessible and above all inclusive; and finally, in point four, we find motivation, which concentrates on not dropping out of the process, enriching the virtual environment with creative and attractive activities that allow the user to remain connected with the space. The virtual learning environment that supports the ATENTI strategy is designed in a way that is accessible in every sense, with downloadable activities, easy to find links and an internal connection of the site that favours its navigability in all the interactive spaces that are found, the same happens with the spaces for contact and explanation of the strategy and of each of the activities designed.

How would you rate the visual aspect of the virtual learning environment?

On a rating scale of 1 to 5, where 1 is a bad visual aspect and 5 is an excellent visual aspect, my rating is 4.5, because the colours are very well defined, making it attractive for the children and each space generates an intention of exploration. For the AVA we took into account the relation that is given about the psychology of colours where it plays an important role in the creation of learning environments, using it as stimuli facilitators of the process and thanks to them it is possible to attract attention exerting influence on certain actions in the educational context; the colours themselves are defined according to the contexts in which they are used (Ortiz, 2014), and for this case in the educational context they are part of those additional stimuli that favour processes. In the virtual learning environment of the attentional educational strategy ATENTI, the colours were used according to the relation that occurs at each moment of the process (see figure 6), using blue, yellow and red as the predominant colours in the virtual environment, considering this scale as important in the attentional processes of children in general.

Figure 7*The power of colours for children*

Color	Qué transmite	Beneficioso para...
Blanco	Pureza, calma y orden visual	Incentiva la creatividad
Azul	Calma, serenidad	Mejora el sueño. Bueno para niños nerviosos
Rojo	Energía, vitalidad	Ayuda en niños más tímidos
Amarillo	Positivismo, energía	Estimula la concentración. Bueno para niños con depresión
Verde	Equilibrio y calma	Mejora la capacidad lectora
Naranja	Energía y positivismo	Estimula la comunicación
Morado	Tranquilidad y misterio	Potencia la intuición

Colour	What it conveys	Beneficial for...
White	Purity, calm and visual order	Encourage creativity
Blue	Calm, serenity	Improves sleep. Good for nervous children
Red	Energy, vrt ality	Help for shy children
	Positivism, energy	Stimulates concentration. Good for children with disabilities.
Green	Balance y calm	Improving reading skills
Orange	Energy y positivism	Stimulates communication
Purple	Tranquility y mystery	Empowering intuition

Gufainiantii.com 2019.

/Does the virtual learning environment support digital learning of content?

In all learning processes, different processes converge between the environment, the individual and the media, generating cognitive impacts in the processes of assimilation and accommodation of different moments in the neuroplasticity of the children, as related by (Herrera M., Las fuentes del aprendizaje en ambientes virtuales educativos, 2002), where he evidences the sources of the processes with and without the use of technology to favour the apprehension of contents. The sources of learning in virtual educational environments, 2002), where he evidences the sources of the processes with and without the use of technology to favour the apprehension of contents,

Figure 8 *Non-computerised* **sources**

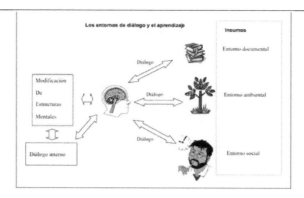

Figure 9Sources *with computer use*

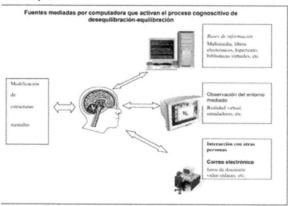

understanding these sources, the fact that with the help of virtual learning environments, the contribution of knowledge is easier, and even more so in the attentional context that corresponds within the pedagogical strategy, therefore ATENTI completely favours the acquisition of new cognitive concepts, takes on more strength.

('.Additional comments?

For better organisation I would suggest more tabs, so that all the content is not on a single page as it is very interesting all the content, which could be seen more organised in tabs, but in general the content is easy to see and easy to find.

In conclusion, within the first validation of the AVA, it specifically meets the necessary requirements to validate its use within the strategy, complying with the parameters of content, accessibility, resources and in general terms its interaction space, being a warm learning environment, where the child and his or her parents can navigate in an easy and safe way, contributing the contents to their attentional processes from the educational and formative context in any place. The virtual environment provides all the tools for the introduction to the strategy, access to the contents of each of the activities, important, updated and accurate information on the general conditions of Attention Deficit Disorder and as a fundamental plus, a contact area with the creators and technical support of the virtual environment, which guarantees a transparent and dynamic process.

VPA 2 Validation

The second expert, a lecturer at the education secretariat's in-service training centre, with a master's degree in educational technologies.

gIs the learning environment intuitive?

Yes, it is practical and easily accessible. A virtual environment is described as intuitive, when it allows support in flexible environments giving the possibility of easy and safe access, where individual and collective development of knowledge is encouraged (Solan & Marianela, 2009). From there, the technological needs are established to articulate the contents with the process of the virtual learning environment, which defines a precision within the strategy that fully complies with both pedagogical and technological pretensions.

g Is the content organised to promote understanding?

Yes, it is very well structured and organised, the process is understood for each of the sessions and the explanatory videos facilitate the understanding of each activity. VPAs are designed for users, opening up points of connection between participants and the virtual space, unifying integrated systems of different purposes with specific objectives (Angel, 2017), the organisation of content is fundamental when generating technological spaces in a virtual learning environment, due to the premise that it is designed for any type of population or user, and, in particular, the ATENTI strategy organises its activities according to the premises established in the creation of virtuality, taking great care with the articulation of links and content, making it organised and easy to understand in the different spaces available in the virtual environment.

/Is the VPA user-friendly (navigation, resources, icons, material)?

Yes, it is very easy to access and the navigation on the platform is pleasant and motivates with each of its spaces to continue exploring it. Every virtual learning environment must have pedagogical, technological, curricular and strategic elements, this touching on the construction of the virtual space, but it must also have other elements such as teaching and learning strategy, objects of study, didactics and theories that facilitate the pedagogical and virtual processes, these elements guarantee a suitable environment, capable of favouring each of the contents and its navigability (Saza, 2018). In the structuring and articulation of the pedagogical strategy with the virtual learning environment, the elements were taken into account to facilitate to a greater extent its use and management within all the virtual pages and spaces, guaranteeing a general appropriation and closing the space of desertion due to complexity in the application.

/On the visual aspect, how would you rate the virtual learning environment?

On a rating scale of 1 to 5, where 1 is a bad visual aspect and 5 is an excellent visual aspect, the expert's rating was 4.5. The visual aspect in children with attentional difficulties plays a fundamental role when involving them in a virtual strategy, since, due to their disruptive behaviour, each case presents variable behavioural alterations, being fundamental that the child recognises at this stage of his or her life activities and learning instances linked to the game that favour their cognitive development (Godoy & Diaz, 2016), therefore, it is fundamental that the participant is able to recognise the visual aspect of the game in a way that favours their cognitive development (Godoy & Diaz, 2016). Diaz, 2016), therefore, it is essential that the participant is "hooked" from the first moment with the virtual environment, and the visual aspect fulfils in this sense with the appropriate parameters to establish an assertive relationship between the process and the child.

gDoes the virtual learning environment support digital learning of content?

Yes, thanks to its design and the organisation of information. In the integration of teaching-learning processes with technologies, a more open contact has been generated in the development of processes that demand more and more autonomy and independence of the user in the development of activities, requiring a more autonomous appropriation of realities and knowledge from the pedagogical point of view (Rodrigue/. & Barragan, 2017), therefore, they begin to discriminate the cognitive functions of the apprehension of knowledge according to the external and internal stimuli that take place in exploration of the contents of the virtual environment, generating sensory stimuli that for this case applies as it is the attention (Herrera M., 2018),

Figure *10New technologies and their executive functions*

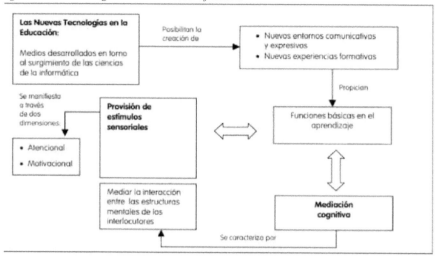

The digital apprehension of the content supported in the virtual environment, favours the attentional stimuli that gives rise to the ATENTI pedagogical strategy, therefore, as the contents are clear and organised, they comply with the mediation of knowledge supported by the new technologies.
¿Additional remarks?

A very good job, very nice design of the platform, easy access and navigation. Concluding the validation of the second expert in the technological aspect, the favourability of the virtual environment is approved, within the process of the pedagogical strategy, since it fulfils the parameters of organisation of contents, accessibility, navigability and finally with all the components mentioned so that it is a safe and friendly environment for all the participants. All the components of the virtual space are designed under an interface that provides pleasant stimuli for the children participants with an instructional model according to the requirements of the strategy and that complies with the parameters of construction of a virtual learning environment.

6 Conclusions

The attentional processes as a cognitive stimulus are fundamental when it comes to being able to develop daily activities in children, achieving adherence to the disciplinary parameters of each context, which is why they are so important and relevant in the educational environment, an environment that, together with the family context, makes the greatest contribution to the development of neuroplasticity and other neuronal processes that will guide the condition that develops when they are children for the rest of their lives; Within the attentional difficulties of ADHD, the importance of having an early detection and an adequate approach within the first years of life is highlighted, with the purpose of advancing and strengthening the cognitive processes in which the child has difficulty in the educational context. In order to contribute to the attentional processes of children with signs of ADHD, the ATENTI pedagogical-attentional strategy was born, which in the first phase validated both the contents and the virtual learning environment and in the second phase was implemented with children of cycle 1 of the IED Bravo Paez.

The research in phase I, faces a validation from two perspectives, the first validation of the pedagogical content and the second, validation of the virtual learning environment or work interface, having in each perspective two experts, who on the side of the pedagogical component are psychologists experts in attentional processes and for the technological case, two teachers trained in virtual processes.

Concretising the functionalities of the pedagogical processes within the strategy, a validation is framed in all its aspects, since the correspondence of the purpose, which is to strengthen the attentional processes of the children, with the content is evident, allowing a bridge between the particular pretensions of each case involved, The fact that the medium through which the strategy is carried out is a virtual learning environment, which shows the importance and impact of technology in current processes, especially in working with children, is also considered positive. There is a correlation between the theoretical and practical contents for the educational aspect, affirming the relationship that is evident, since each activity is very well supported theoretically with clear and reliable information, which makes the strategy timely and valid to be developed in the educational context and with the target population. The validation and pedagogical execution is carried out in a concrete way, approving all the involved topics of contents and pertinence within the strategy, starting with a very explanatory video of the same, and likewise, of each stage of the process in the own content of the sessions.

For the technological aspect, an intuitive virtual environment is validated, with organised and easy to access and understand content, downloadable content and online work, which allows, as related to the planning and construction processes of a VPA, a simple exploration and easy accessibility of content, Furthermore, its navigation, interface resources and its visual aspect are validated, which in this case was taken as a reference to the psychoiography of colours, which guarantees in every aspect the investigation of the process, without leaving a single detail to the subjective appreciation of the user. In short, all the validated aspects approve a correct apprehension of the digital knowledge and the appropriation of knowledge of the participants in the strategy, by activating the cognitive processes necessary for the improvement of attention in the educational field once the fieldwork is developed.

In conclusion, the strategy supported in the virtual learning environment, is validated in its totality by the experts, being understood as the fundamental process for the planning of the investigation that will favour many contexts, contributing contents and social work as support to the social educational investigation, that in its pedagogical and virtual content complies with a rigorous study of each one of its components, with the purpose that the strategy is as reliable as possible and achieves the necessary impact in the attentional processes.

In the second phase of the work, it is concluded that the attentional process that frames the strategy is ideal and approves with the objectives in its totality, which is manifested in the results of comparison by means of the tests of entrance and exit of the process, achieving an adaptability in time, in basic abilities, speed of psychomotor processing, executive functions, inhibition capacity, sequencing, focalisation, and all the types of attention, all the above by means of the already mentioned neuroplasticity, which frames the specific stfmulus of the strategy, executive functions, inhibition capacity, sequencing, focalisation, and all types of attention, all of the above by means of the aforementioned neuroplasticity, which frames the specific stimulus and converts it into a new network of neuronal connections and adapts to the new context of attentional needs, improving everyday processes.

It is still worth highlighting that in the process of implementation, which lasted four weeks and consisted of a month of work and new stimuli, the acceptance not only in the participation was important, but emanates from a latent need of the parents to look for ways out and points of support for the daily situations that are framed as difficult for their children, Among them, the educational moment, which is perhaps one of the most complex to handle, as it requires the joint and articulated support of the interdisciplinary medical team, the family and the teacher, in order to direct actions towards their integrated development, starting from the particularities that the disorder may cause.

Although it is known that the disorder is very particular in each case, and touching only the attentional concept, institutions such as the Development and Childhood Foundation state that the work should be carried out without pause for at least 6 months to 18 months depending on the progress and prescriptions of the child, and it is recommended that the activity be linked to the annual work plan of the institution in order to continue the progress of the processes; On the other hand, and contributing to what was previously established, in the comparative results we observe that child 4 and child 8 show a significant improvement, this is due to the fact that in their particular cases, they have the work and follow-up of an interdisciplinary medical team (ionoaudiology, occupational therapy and psychology), which further affirms the importance of the ATENTI pedagogical strategy in the attentional development of children with signs or diagnosed with ADHD.

For education it is an unbeatable opportunity to create pedagogical strategies with such a social impact as ATENTI, due to the fact that its implementation in subsequent phases will bring about improvements in children in a considerable way, understanding the urgency of an early approach that does not generate costs, that is to say that it is inclusive of any type of population and socio-economic stratum.

Finally, under article 77 of the General Education Law, which grants schools the autonomy to organise their curricula and adjust their PEI according to the needs of the context, and the Ministry of National Education in Decree 1290, where schools have the power to define their general evaluation system, with the fundamental purpose of being able to adjust the contents of early childhood to the structure of the strategy in contexts where attentional difficulties are defined as a risk factor in the educational processes, understanding this as an idealism that will be reflected as the strategy covers more educational institutions.

References

Aidyne (2018). Evaluation of attention. *Centre for psychoneurocognitive care, teaching and research.*

Alvarez, C. (2012). La relación teoria-practica en los procesos de ensenanza-aprendizaje. *Educatio Siglo XXI.*

Angel, A. (2017). Conceptualization of Virtual Learning Environments. *digitk.*

Aznar, S., & Webster, T. (2009). Physical activity and health in childhood and adolescence. *General Technical Secretariat. Publications Centre. Ministry of Education and Science.*

Balbuena, A., Barrio, E., Gonzalez, C., Pedrosa, B., Rodnguez, C., & Yaguez, L. (2014). *Protocol for the detection and evaluation of students with Attention Deficit and Hyperactivity Disorder in the educational environment.* Department of Education, Culture and Sport.

Ballesteros, s. (2014). Selective attention modulates information processing and implicit memory. *Scielo.*

Buzon, O. (2005). La incorporacion de las platafornas virtuales a la ensenanza: una experiencia de formación on-line basada en competencias. *Revista Latinoamericana de iecnDlogi'a educativa.*

Caamano, C. (2018). Keys to enhance Attention/Concentration. *CeACS.*

Carriedo, A. (2014). Benefits of Physical Education in students diagnosed with Attention Deficit Hyperactivity Disorder
with Attention Deficit Hyperactivity Disorder (ADHD). *Journal of Sport and Health Research.*

Cedeno, E. (2019). Virtual learning environments and their innovative role in the teaching process. *Journal of Humanities and Social Sciences.*

Cobo, C. (2016). *La Innovation Pendiente. Reflexiones (y Provocaciones) sobre education, iecno'logi'a y conocimiento.* Montevideo: Editorial Sudamericana Uruguaya S.A.

Crichton, A. (1798). *An inquiry into the nature and origin of mental derangement.* London: Bibliotheck.

Crisol, E., & Campos, M. N. (2019). Rehabilitation of executive functions in 6-year-old children with ADHD. a case study. *Revista de curriculum y formacion del profesorado*, 295, 296.

De la Pena, F., Palacio, J., & Barragan, E. (2010). Declaration de Cartagena for Attention Deficit Hyperactivity Disorder (ADHD): breaking the stigma. *Rev. Sci. Health*, 95.

Eltiempo (06 October 2014). Bogota is a city full of hyperactive children, study concludes. *El Tiempo.*

Estevez, B. (2015). *The educational inclusion of students with ADD/ADHD breaking curricular and organizational barriers in primary schools.* Granada: University of Granada.

Flores, E. (2016). Process of attention and its implication in the learning process. *Didasc@lia: Didactics and Education.*

Francia, A., Migues, M., & Penalver, Y. (2018). Attention deficit hyperactivity disorder, some considerations in its diagnosis and treatment. *Rev acta medica centro.*

Fundacioncadah.org (2012). ADHD and perceptual-motor problems. *Fundacion Cadah org.*

Gamboa, M. C., Garaa, Y., & Marlen, B. (2013). Pedagogical and didactic strategies for the development of multiple intelligences and autonomous learning. *UNAD.*

Garces, m., & Suarez, J. (2014). Neuroplasticity: biochemical and neurophysiological aspects. *ESC medicine.*

Garces, M., & Suarez, J. (2014). Neuroplasticity: biochemical and neurophysiological aspects. *ESC med.*

Garcia, M., & De la torre, M. (16 December 2013). RESPONSE TIME OSCILLATIONS AND THEIR RELATION TO MEASURES OF INATTENTION IN CHILDREN WITH ATTENTION DEFICIT HYPERACTIVITY DISORDER. *THE RESPONSE TIME OSCILLATIONS AND THEIR RELATION TO MEASURES OF INATTENTION IN CHILDREN WITH ATTENTION DEFICIT HYPERACTIVITY DISORDER.* Madrid, Spain: Universidad Autonoma de Madrid.

Godoy, P., & D^az, J. (2016). *Necesidades educalivas especiales asociadas a problemas de atencion y concentration.* Santiago de Chile: Atenas Ltda.

Herguedas, M. (2016). PSYCHOMOTOR INTERVENTION IN CHILDREN. CONTRAST BETWEEN ATTENTION DEFICIT DISORDER AND HYPERACTIVITY. *Doctoral thesis.* Valladolid, Spain.

Hergueras, M. d. (2016). *Psychomotor intervention in children with attention deficit hyperactivity disorder.* Valladolid: University of Valladolid.

Hernandez, R., Fernandez, C., & Baptista, P. (2010). *Metodolog^a de la Investigation.* Mexico: McGrawHill.

Hernandez, S. (2013). Thesis seminar. *Uaeh.*

Herrera, M. (2002). The sources of learning in virtual educational environments. *Revista Iberoamericana de education principal OEI.*

Herrera, M. (2018). Considerations for the didactic design of virtual learning environments: a proposal based on the cognitive functions of learning. *Iberoamerican Journal of Education.*

Herrera, M. (2018). Considerations for the didactic design of virtual learning environments: a proposal based on the cognitive functions of learning. *Iberoamerican journal of education.*

Hidalgo, M., & Sanchez, L. (2014). Attention deficit hyperactivity disorder. Clinical manifestations and evolution. Diagnosis from the scientific evidence. *Pediatria Integral*, 611, 612.

Hueso, A., & Cascant, M. (2012). *Melodology and quantitative research techniques.* Valencia: Universitat Politecnica de Valencia.

Jimenez, G., Jose, V., & Restrepo, F. (2019). Interference management in attention deficit hyperactivity disorder (ADHD): review. *Ces psicologia.*

THE MOTOR SKILLS OF STUDENTS DIAGNOSED WITH MOTOR IMPAIRMENT. ATTENTION DEFICIT HYPERACTIVITY DISORDER (ADHD), THROUGH THE PRACTICE OF PHYSICAL EDUCATION. (n.d.).

Lange C, R. S. (30 November 2010). U.*S. National Library of Medicine.* Retrieved from https://www.ncbi.nlm.nih.gov/pmc/articles/PMC3000907/

Llanos, L., Garcia, D., Gonzalez, H., & Puentes, p. (2019). Attention deficit hyperactivity disorder (ADHD) in school children aged 6 to 17 years. *Pediatrics Attention Primary.*

Lopez, A., Ledesma, R., & Escalera, s. (2009). Virtual learning environments. *Ilce.*

Lopez, L. (2018). *Educar la atencion como entrenar esta habilidad en ninos y adultos.* Barcelona: Plataforma actual.

Lopez, P., & fachelli, s. (2015). *Melodology of quantitative social research.* Barcelona, Spain: UAB.

Loro, M., Quintero, Gracia, N., Jimenez, B., Pando, F., Varela, P., ... cORREAS, j. (2009). Actualization in the treatment of attention deficit/hyperactivity disorder. *Neurol.*

Maganto, C., & Cruz, S. (2018). Physical and psychomotor development in infancy. *Physical and psychomotor development in early childhood*, 4-25.

Marchan, M., & Mera, O. (2020). The motor skills of students diagnosed with attention deficit hyperactivity disorder (ADHD) through physical education practice. *Cognosis.*

Mena. (2017). Intervencion desde el ambito escolar en el TDAH. *Departament de psicologia evolutiva I didactics.*

Mena B, N. R. (2006). *El alumno con TDAH Trastorno por déficit de atencion con o sin hiperactividad.* Barcelona: Mayo.

Mena, B., Nicolau, R., Salat, L., Tort, P., & Romero, B. (2006). *The student with ADHD.* Barcelona: Mayo ediciones.

Morales, J. C., & Rodrigue/., S. A. (2018). *ICT, innovation in the classroom and its impacts on higher education.* Bogota: Colombian Association of Educators-Ascolde.

Munoz, H. (2016). Technological mediations: New scenario of pedagogical practice. *Praxis & Saber*, 201-204.

42

Ocampo, A. (2011). The educational context and attentional processes: an approach from culture, emotions and the body. *Journal of education and thought*, 12.

Oliva, H. (2016). Gamification as a methodological strategy in the university educational context. *Reality and reflection.*

Ortiz, G. (2014). Colour. A didactic facilitator. *Journal of psychology .*

Pinto, V., Melia, A., & Miranda (2009). Effects on the family context of a complex psychosocial intervention in children with ADHD. *Escritos de Psicologia.*

Portela, A., Carbonell, M., Hechavarria, M., & Jacas, C. (2016). Attention deficit hyperactivity disorder: some considerations on its etiopathogenesis and treatment. *Medisan.*

Quintanar, Gomez, Solovieva, & Bonilla (2011). Neuropsychological characteristics of preschool children with attention deficit hyperactivity disorder. *Revista CES Psicologia*, 28.

Quintero, F. (2019). Actualizacion en el manejo del TDAH . *aepap.*

Quintero, J., & Castano, C. (2014). Introduction and etiopathogenesis of attention deficit hyperactivity disorder (ADHD). *Pediatna Integral*, 600.

Rincon, C. (2010). La organización escolar por ciclos. An experience of pedagogical transformation in Bogota. *Education and humanism.*

Rodnguez, E. N. (2006). School and attention deficit disorder with/without hyperactivity (ADHD). *Rev Pediatr Aten Primaria*, 178.

Rodnguez, F., & Raul, S. (2015). Gamification, How to motivate your students and improve the classroom climate. *Digiltal-text.*

Rodnguez, M. (2014). Attentional and educational function alterations in multiple sclerosis.
In *Alteraciones atencionales y de la función educativa en esclerosis multiple.*

Rodnguez, M. d., & Barragan, H. (2017). Virtual learning environments as a support to face-to-face teaching to enhance the educational process. *Killkana Social.*

Rohde, L., Buitelaar, J., Gerlach, M., & Faraone, S. (2019). *The global ADHD federation, GU1A.* Sao Paulo: Atmed.

Ruiz, B., Luque, T., & Sanchez, F. (2020). *STROOP test of colours and words.* Madrid: Tea.

Salamanca L, N. M. (2014). Intra-rater reliability of the questionnaire for activity limitations and participation restrictions in children with ADHD. *Revista Colombiana de Psiquiatria*, 26.

Salgado, C. (2007). Investigacion cualitativa: Disenos, evaluación del rigor metodologico y retos. *Dialnet*, 73.

Saza, I. (2018). Propuesta didactica para ambientes virtuales de aprendizaje desde el enfoque praxeologico. *Praxis & Saber.*

Serres, M. (2014). *Thumbelina.* Buenos Aires: Fondo de cultura economica.

Solan, A., & Marianela, D. (2009). Creative didactic strategies in virtual environments for learning. *Actualidades Investigativas en Educacion.*

Suarez, O. (2017). *ADHD and PASS Cognitive Processes.* Spain: University of Vigo.

tdah, C. (2012). *CADAH Foundation.* Retrieved from
https://www.fundacioncadah.org/web/articulo/tdah-actividad-fisica-deportes.html

Tomas, J., & Almenara, J. (2008). Cognitive development: Piaget's and Vygotsky's theories. *Col Legi Oficial de Psi'colegs de Catalunya.*

UNID. (2010). Types of attention . *UNID Basic Psychological Processes*, 3,4 .

Vaquerizo, J. (2005). Hyperactivity in the preschool child: clinical description. *Neurol*, 25.

Velez, A., Talero, C., Gonzalez, R., & Ibanez, M. (2008). Prevalence of attention deficit hyperactivity disorder in school students in Bogota, Colombia. *Neurol COLOMBIA.*

Vinas, M. (2018). The importance of the use of educational platforms. *Letras.*

Annexes

Annex a *Main Virtual Learning Environment* **interface**

Annex *bInterface Information to Parents*

Annex *cInterface Downloadable Support Material*

Annex *dInterface ATENTI Activities*

Annex *eContact interface*

Annex *fRegistration and Login* **Interface**

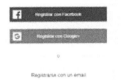

Annex *gActivity 2 Support Monday*

Annex *hActivity 2 Support Tuesday*

Actividad 2: Atentiactividad

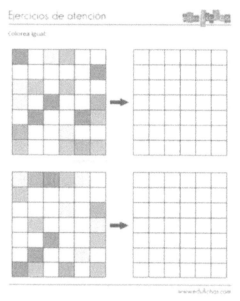

Annex *iActivity 2 Support Wednesday*

Actividad 2: Atentiactividad

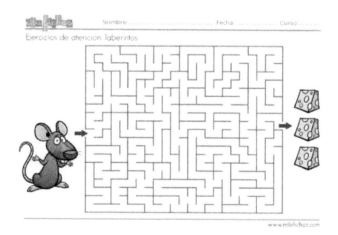

Annex *jActivity 2 Support Thursday*

Actividad 2: Atentiactividad

Annex kActivity 2Support Friday

Actividad 2: Atentiactividad

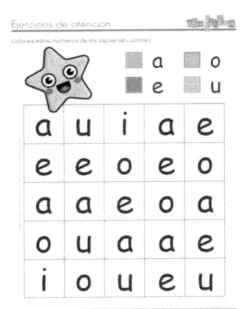

Annex *lMempas* **platform**, *STROPP test and TMT tracking test - pretest and post test*

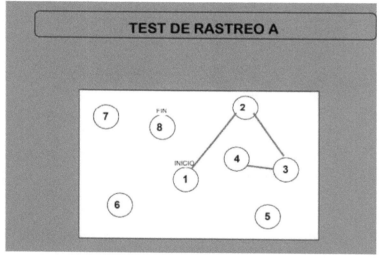

TEST DE RASTREO A

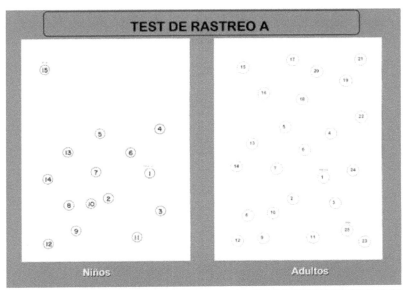

Niños   Adultos

TEST DE RASTREO B

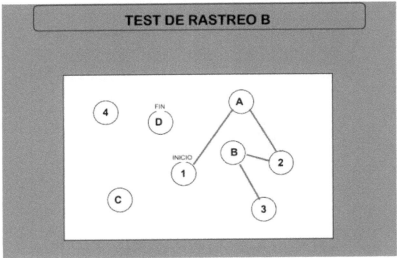

51

TEST DE RASTREO B

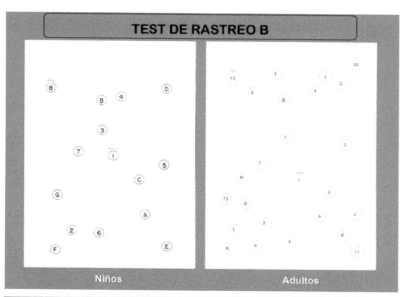

Niños | Adultos

Test de Stroop

ROJO	AZUL	VERDE	ROJO	AZUL
VERDE	VERDE	ROJO	AZUL	VERDE
AZUL	ROJO	AZUL	VERDE	ROJO
VERDE	AZUL	ROJO	ROJO	AZUL
ROJO	ROJO	VERDE	AZUL	VERDE

Resistencia a la interferencia

Annex *mConsent of acceptance of the process*

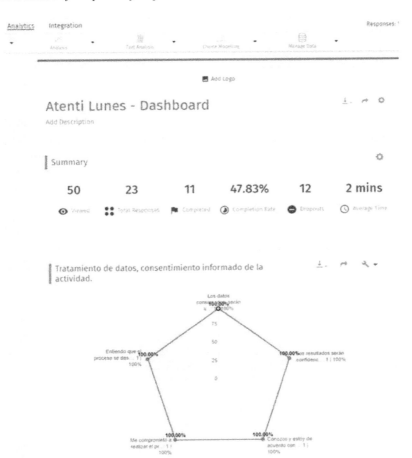

Question	Count	Score	Acepto
Los datos consignados, serán utilizados únicamente para propósitos académicos y dentro de la investigación.			
Los resultados serán confidenciales, solo se podrán utilizar dentro del proceso académico		1	
Conozco y estoy de acuerdo con el proceso que se desarrollará con mi hijo/a		1	

Los datos consignados, serán utilizados únicamente para propósitos académicos y dentro de la investigación.

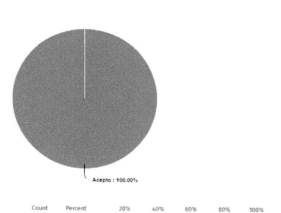

Acepto : 100.00%

Answer	Count	Percent	20%	40%	60%	80%	100%

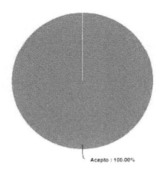

Acepto : 100.00%

Answer		Count	Percent	20%	40%	60%	80%	100%

Conozco y estoy de acuerdo con el proceso que se desarrollará con mi hijo/a.

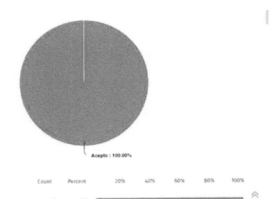

Acepto : 100.00%

Answer	Count	Percent	20%	40%	60%	80%	100%
Acepto	10	100%					

Me comprometo a realizar el proceso de manera veraz
siguiendo los parámetros establecidos por los investigadores.

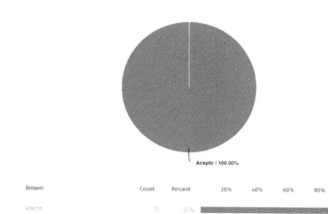

Acepto : 100.00%

Answer	Count	Percent	20%	40%	60%	80%	100%
Acepto	13	100%					

Entiendo que el proceso se desarrollara en su totalidad de
maneta virtual.

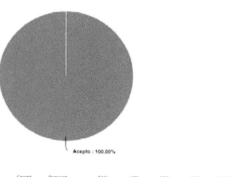

Acepto : 100.00%

Answer	Count	Percent	20%	40%	60%	80%	100%
Acepto	13	100%					

Annex n *Outline of survey and follow-up by session*

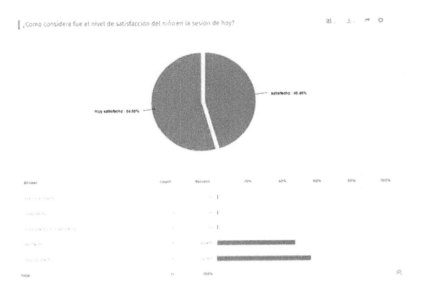

¿Como considera fue el nivel de satisfacción del niño en la sesión de hoy?

¿Recomendarías la actividad del día de hoy?

■: 100.00%

Answer	Count	Percent	20%	40%	60%	80%	100%
Total		100%					

¿Cuántas actividades realizo?

Powered by AI

Question	Count	Score	No realizo	incompleta	completa
	Average	2.91			

¿Qué actividad le gusto más?

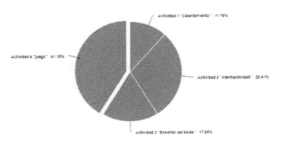

Answer	Count	Percent	20%	40%	60%	80%	100%

¿Qué actividad realizó con mayor facilidad?

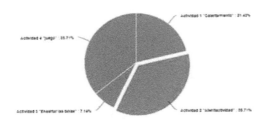

Answer	Count	Percent	20%	40%	60%	80%	100%

¿Qué actividad realizó con mayor dificultad?

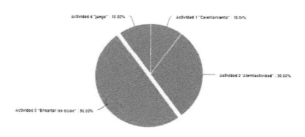

Answer	Count	Percent	20%	40%	60%	80%	100%
Actividad 1 "Calentamiento"		10%					
Actividad 2 "Atentlactividad"		30%					
Actividad 3 "Ensartar las bolas"		90%					
Actividad 4 "Juego"		10%					

Duración de cada actividad

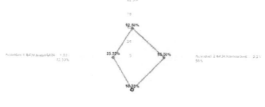

Powered by AI

Question	Count	Score	1 a 2 minutos	3 a 4 minutos	5 a 6 minutos	7 a 8 minutos
Actividad 1 "Calentamiento"						
Actividad 2 "Atentlactividad"						
Actividad 3 "Ensartar las bolas"						
Actividad 4 "Juego"						

Tiempo total de la actividad

Comentarios de la actividad

Milton Keynes UK
Ingram Content Group UK Ltd.
UKHW040833120224
437701UK00001B/110